VITAL RECORD KEEPING MADE E-Z

MADE E-Z PRODUCTS, Inc.
Deerfield Beach, Florida / www.MadeE-Z.com

NOTICE:

THIS PRODUCT IS NOT INTENDED TO PROVIDE LEGAL ADVICE. IT CONTAINS GENERAL INFORMATION FOR EDUCATIONAL PURPOSES ONLY. PLEASE CONSULT AN ATTORNEY IN ALL LEGAL MATTERS. THIS PRODUCT WAS NOT PREPARED BY A PERSON LICENSED TO PRACTICE LAW IN THIS STATE.

Vital Record Keeping Made E-Z™
Copyright 2000 Made E-Z Products, Inc.
Printed in the United States of America

MADE E-Z
PRODUCTS

384 South Military Trail
Deerfield Beach, FL 33442
Tel. 954-480-8933
Fax 954-480-8906

http://www.MadeE-Z.com
All rights reserved.

1 2 3 4 5 6 7 8 9 10   CPC   R 10 9 8 7 6 5 4 3 2

This publication is designed to provide accurate and authoritative information in regard to subject matter covered. It is sold with the understanding that neither the publisher nor author is engaged in rendering legal, accounting, or other professional services. If legal advice or other expert assistance is required, the services of a competent professional should be sought. From: *A Declaration of Principles jointly adopted by a Committee of the American Bar Association and a Committee of Publishers.*

Vital Record Keeping Made E-Z

Limited warranty and disclaimer

This self-help product is intended to be used by the consumer for his/her own benefit. It may not be reproduced in whole or in part, resold or used for commercial purposes without written permission from the publisher. In addition to copyright violations, the unauthorized reproduction and use of this product to benefit a second party may be considered the unauthorized practice of law.

This product is designed to provide authoritative and accurate information in regard to the subject matter covered. However, the accuracy of the information is not guaranteed, as laws and regulations may change or be subject to differing interpretations. Consequently, you may be responsible for following alternative procedures, or using material or forms different from those supplied with this product. It is strongly advised that you examine the laws of your state before acting upon any of the material contained in this product.

As with any matter, common sense should determine whether you need the assistance of an attorney. We urge you to consult with an attorney, qualified estate planner, or tax professional, or to seek any other relevant expert advice whenever substantial sums of money are involved, you doubt the suitability of the product you have purchased, or if there is anything about the product that you do not understand including its adequacy to protect you. Even if you are completely satisfied with this product, we encourage you to have your attorney review it.

Neither the author, publisher, distributor nor retailer are engaged in rendering legal, accounting or other professional services. Accordingly, the publisher, author, distributor and retailer shall have neither liability nor responsibility to any party for any loss or damage caused or alleged to be caused by the use of this product.

Copyright Notice

The purchaser of this guide is hereby authorized to reproduce in any form or by any means, electronic or mechanical, including photocopying, all forms and documents contained in this guide, provided it is for non-profit, educational or private use. Such reproduction requires no further permission from the publisher and/or payment of any permission fee.

The reproduction of any form or document in any other publication intended for sale is prohibited without the written permission of the publisher. Publication for nonprofit use should provide proper attribution to Made E-Z Products.

Table of contents

Introduction to Vital Record Keeping Made E-Z™

Now you can organize your personal life as efficiently as you can your business life with the help of *Vital Record Keeping Made E-Z*.

More than 200 forms have been assembled into a comprehensive recordkeeping system called *Vital Record Keeping Made E-Z*, designed to simplify the life of you and your family. This basic, easy-to-use book contains virtually every form you will ever need to keep your life running smoothly, from travel planning to family event scheduling to monthly goal setting.

Vital Record Keeping Made E-Z is the ultimate record-maintenance system, designed to locate and organize vital financial, personal, legal, family and household information quickly and conveniently. This book helps you create a permanent record of vital data that encompasses every aspect of your life, and is easy to maintain and update. The forms it contains are easy to understand, ready to use, flexible, and suited to your individual and family needs.

There are a number of ways *Vital Record Keeping Made E-Z* will prove valuable to you. It can help eliminate time-consuming record searching, help you maintain important personal and family records, give you the tools essential for effective planning, and assist you in managing your finances.

Vital Record Keeping Made E-Z is divided into eleven sections, each designed to help organize a certain aspect of your life:

Section 1   **Family/Personal Records** contains forms to help organize everything from your grocery list and babysitting expenses to your volunteer record.

Section 2   **Business Forms** assists you in organizing your personal business activities through forms such as a long distance phone call record, home office product order form and advertising budget.

Section 3   **Educational Records** tracks your scholastic achievements from grade school years through educational courses taken beyond college.

Section 4   **Health Records** compiles all health care-related documents, including doctor visits and health insurance policies.

Section 5   **Investments/Financial Records** helps organize your personal finances by compiling all your financial records, from certificates of deposit to zero coupon bonds.

Section 6   **Purchase and Maintenance Records** helps you keep track of products ordered and products to order. Other forms organize home and vehicle maintenance records.

Section 7   **Important Names, Dates and Facts** never lets you forget another birthday or anniversary. Important names, events and phone numbers are easily accessible when you complete these forms.

Section 8   **Event Planning** assists you in organizing your next social gathering. Plan your next Christmas party or special dinner with the help of these forms.

Section 9   **Travel Data** covers all the travel information you'll need to plan and prepare upcoming business or social trips.

Section 10   **Recreational Activities** compiles forms to keep records of your hobbies or special interests.

Section 11   **Special Projects** makes it easier to accomplish your goals by listing objectives and updating project ideas.

Using the forms provided in all eleven sections will lead you to become more organized and efficient in all areas of your life.

Let *Vital Record Keeping Made E-Z* become a part of your daily routine and establish a more organized lifestyle for you and your family.

FORM DIRECTORY

Forms by section

Section 1

Section 2

Section 3
Educational Records..*95*

Section 4
Health Records...*109*

Section 5

Section 6
Purchase and Maintenance Records...........................*183*

Section 7
Important Names, Dates and Facts............................*203*

Section 8
Event Planning *221*

Section 9
Travel Data.. *237*

Section 10

Section 11

Family/
personal
records

1

Section 1

Family/personal records

Forms in this section

ALIMONY/SUPPORT PAYMENTS

Name: _____

Amount Sent/Received	Date Sent/Received	Amount In Arrears	Next Payment Due
$_____	_____	$_____	_____
$_____	_____	$_____	_____
$_____	_____	$_____	_____
$_____	_____	$_____	_____
$_____	_____	$_____	_____
$_____	_____	$_____	_____
$_____	_____	$_____	_____
$_____	_____	$_____	_____
$_____	_____	$_____	_____
$_____	_____	$_____	_____
$_____	_____	$_____	_____
$_____	_____	$_____	_____
$_____	_____	$_____	_____
$_____	_____	$_____	_____
$_____	_____	$_____	_____
$_____	_____	$_____	_____
$_____	_____	$_____	_____
$_____	_____	$_____	_____
$_____	_____	$_____	_____
$_____	_____	$_____	_____
$_____	_____	$_____	_____

| $_____ | | $_____ | |
| **Total** | | **Total** | |

APPAREL SIZING CHART

Name:_____ Date:_____ Measurements:_____

    Blouse_____ Shoes _____ Hat_____

    Dress_____ Shirt _____ Suit _____

    Belt _____ Skirt _____ Pants _____

    Slip _____ Vest_____ Coat_____

    Jacket _____ Gloves _____ Other _____

Name:_____ Date:_____ Measurements:_____

    Blouse_____ Shoes _____ Hat_____

    Dress_____ Shirt _____ Suit _____

    Belt _____ Skirt _____ Pants _____

    Slip _____ Vest_____ Coat_____

    Jacket _____ Gloves _____ Other _____

Name:_____ Date:_____ Measurements:_____

    Blouse_____ Shoes _____ Hat_____

    Dress_____ Shirt _____ Suit _____

    Belt _____ Skirt _____ Pants _____

    Slip _____ Vest_____ Coat_____

    Jacket _____ Gloves _____ Other _____

Name:_____ Date:_____ Measurements:_____

    Blouse_____ Shoes _____ Hat_____

    Dress_____ Shirt _____ Suit _____

    Belt _____ Skirt _____ Pants _____

    Slip _____ Vest_____ Coat_____

    Jacket _____ Gloves _____ Other _____

AUTOMOBILE RECORD

Vehicle Information

Make of Car: _____ Model: _____ Year:_____

Vehicle ID Number: _____ License Number:_____

Annual Registration Number:_____ Expiration:_____

Title Holder: _____

Vehicle Insurance

Insurance Company:_____

Policy Number: _____ Deductible:_____

Coverages: _____

_____

Premium: _____ Due: _____

Agent: _____

Address: _____

_____

Phone/Fax Number:_____

Vehicle Information

Make of Car: _____ Model: _____ Year:_____

Vehicle ID Number: _____ License Number:_____

Annual Registration Number:_____ Expiration:_____

Title Holder: _____

Vehicle Insurance

Insurance Company:_____

Policy Number: _____ Deductible:_____

Coverages: _____

_____

Premium: _____ Due: _____

Agent: _____

Address: _____

_____

Phone/Fax Number:_____

BABY-SITTING EXPENSES

Name: _____

Name of Service	Date	Time Spent	Hours	Rate of Pay	Amount Paid
_____	_____	_____	_____	$ _____	$ _____
_____	_____	_____	_____	$ _____	$ _____
_____	_____	_____	_____	$ _____	$ _____
_____	_____	_____	_____	$ _____	$ _____
_____	_____	_____	_____	$ _____	$ _____
_____	_____	_____	_____	$ _____	$ _____
_____	_____	_____	_____	$ _____	$ _____
_____	_____	_____	_____	$ _____	$ _____
_____	_____	_____	_____	$ _____	$ _____
_____	_____	_____	_____	$ _____	$ _____
_____	_____	_____	_____	$ _____	$ _____
_____	_____	_____	_____	$ _____	$ _____
_____	_____	_____	_____	$ _____	$ _____
_____	_____	_____	_____	$ _____	$ _____
_____	_____	_____	_____	$ _____	$ _____
_____	_____	_____	_____	$ _____	$ _____
_____	_____	_____	_____	$ _____	$ _____
_____	_____	_____	_____	$ _____	$ _____
_____	_____	_____	_____	$ _____	$ _____
_____	_____	_____	_____	$ _____	$ _____
_____	_____	_____	_____	$ _____	$ _____
_____	_____	_____	_____	$ _____	$ _____

Total Hours: _____   Total Paid: $ _____

CHILD CARE SERVICES

Caregiver's Name: _____ Rate:_____

Address:_____ Phone: _____

Days/Hours Available: _____Age: _____

References: _____

Additional Information: _____

_____

Caregiver's Name: _____ Rate:_____

Address:_____ Phone: _____

Days/Hours Available: _____Age: _____

References: _____

Additional Information: _____

_____

Caregiver's Name: _____ Rate:_____

Address:_____ Phone: _____

Days/Hours Available: _____Age: _____

References: _____

Additional Information: _____

_____

Caregiver's Name: _____ Rate:_____

Address:_____ Phone: _____

Days/Hours Available: _____Age: _____

References: _____

Additional Information: _____

_____

COUPON REGISTER

Item	Coupon Amount	Expires
1. _____	$ _____	_____
2. _____	$ _____	_____
3. _____	$ _____	_____
4. _____	$ _____	_____
5. _____	$ _____	_____
6. _____	$ _____	_____
7. _____	$ _____	_____
8. _____	$ _____	_____
9. _____	$ _____	_____
10. _____	$ _____	_____
11. _____	$ _____	_____
12. _____	$ _____	_____
13. _____	$ _____	_____
14. _____	$ _____	_____
15. _____	$ _____	_____
16. _____	$ _____	_____
17. _____	$ _____	_____
18. _____	$ _____	_____
19. _____	$ _____	_____
20. _____	$ _____	_____
21. _____	$ _____	_____
22. _____	$ _____	_____
23. _____	$ _____	_____

DOCUMENT FINDER

Name:_____ Date:_____

Insurance Documents: _____

Birth Certificates:_____

Instructions in Case of Death: _____

Deeds/Proofs of Ownership: _____

Marriage Certificates:_____

Social Security Cards:_____

Military Records:_____

Divorce Decrees: _____

Mortgage Documents: _____

Bank Passbooks: _____

Passports: _____

Tax Returns: _____

Wills and Trusts: _____

Prenuptial Agreements: _____

Business Papers: _____

Death Certificates:_____

Warranties: _____

Stock Certificates: _____

Other Investment Certificates: _____

Letters of Final Request:_____

Organ Donor Authorizations: _____

Citizenship Papers: _____

Safe Deposit Keys:_____

Financial Records: _____

FAMILY CELEBRATIONS

Date	Occasion	Time	Location

FAMILY TREE

Father's Paternal Grandfather	Father's Maternal Grandfather	Mother's Maternal Grandfather	Mother's Paternal Grandfather
_____	_____	_____	_____
_____	_____	_____	_____

Father's Paternal Grandmother	Father's Maternal Grandmother	Mother's Maternal Grandmother	Mother's Paternal Grandmother
_____	_____	_____	_____
_____	_____	_____	_____

Father's Father	Father's Mother	Mother's Father	Mother's Mother
_____	_____	_____	_____
_____	_____	_____	_____

Father's Siblings

_____   _____   _____   _____
_____   _____   _____   _____
_____   _____   _____   _____

Mother's Siblings

Your Paternal Cousins

_____   _____   _____   _____
_____   _____   _____   _____
_____   _____   _____   _____

Your Maternal Cousins

Father	Mother
_____	_____
_____	_____

YOU: _____   SPOUSE: _____

Date of Birth: _____   Date of Birth: _____
Date of Death: _____   Date of Death: _____
Place of Birth: _____   Place of Birth: _____

Your Siblings	Spouse	Your Children	Spouse
_____	_____	_____	_____
_____	_____	_____	_____
_____	_____	_____	_____
_____	_____	_____	_____

Nieces & Nephews	Spouse	Your Grandchildren	Spouse
_____	_____	_____	_____
_____	_____	_____	_____
_____	_____	_____	_____
_____	_____	_____	_____

Form F105

FAVORITE RECIPES

For the Preparation of (Dish): _____

Ingredients   Quantity

_____   _____

_____   _____

_____   _____

_____   _____

_____   _____

_____   _____

_____   _____

_____   _____

_____   _____

Directions: _____

_____

_____

_____

_____

_____

_____

Suggested Accompaniments: _____

_____

Occasions when Served: _____

_____

FAVORITE RESTAURANTS

Restaurant: _____ Phone: _____

Address: _____

Meal/Dish _____ Date: _____

Rating: _____

Restaurant: _____ Phone: _____

Address: _____

Meal/Dish _____ Date: _____

Rating: _____

Restaurant: _____ Phone: _____

Address: _____

Meal/Dish _____ Date: _____

Rating: _____

Restaurant: _____ Phone: _____

Address: _____

Meal/Dish _____ Date: _____

Rating: _____

Restaurant: _____ Phone: _____

Address: _____

Meal/Dish _____ Date: _____

Rating: _____

FORMER ADDRESSES

Name: _____

Dates of Residency: _____ to _____

Address: _____

Leased: _____ Owned: _____ Rented: _____

Name of Landlord: _____ Phone: _____

Address: _____

Dates of Residency: _____ to _____

Address: _____

Leased: _____ Owned: _____ Rented: _____

Name of Landlord: _____ Phone: _____

Address: _____

Dates of Residency: _____ to _____

Address: _____

Leased: _____ Owned: _____ Rented: _____

Name of Landlord: _____ Phone: _____

Address: _____

Dates of Residency: _____ to _____

Address: _____

Leased: _____ Owned: _____ Rented: _____

Name of Landlord: _____ Phone: _____

Address: _____

FREEZER STOCK INVENTORY

Item:	Date	Raw	Blanched	Cooked	Part Cooked
		❏	❏	❏	❏
		❏	❏	❏	❏
		❏	❏	❏	❏
		❏	❏	❏	❏
		❏	❏	❏	❏
		❏	❏	❏	❏
		❏	❏	❏	❏
		❏	❏	❏	❏
		❏	❏	❏	❏
		❏	❏	❏	❏
		❏	❏	❏	❏
		❏	❏	❏	❏
		❏	❏	❏	❏
		❏	❏	❏	❏
		❏	❏	❏	❏
		❏	❏	❏	❏
		❏	❏	❏	❏
		❏	❏	❏	❏
		❏	❏	❏	❏
		❏	❏	❏	❏
		❏	❏	❏	❏
		❏	❏	❏	❏
		❏	❏	❏	❏
		❏	❏	❏	❏
		❏	❏	❏	❏
		❏	❏	❏	❏
		❏	❏	❏	❏
		❏	❏	❏	❏
		❏	❏	❏	❏
		❏	❏	❏	❏
		❏	❏	❏	❏

GIFT THANK-YOU LIST

Received From	Gift	Date Gift Received	Date Thank-You Mailed

GROCERY LIST

Date: _____

Item	Price	Coupon (✓)	Checklist (✓)
1. _____	$ _____	_____	_____
2. _____	$ _____	_____	_____
3. _____	$ _____	_____	_____
4. _____	$ _____	_____	_____
5. _____	$ _____	_____	_____
6. _____	$ _____	_____	_____
7. _____	$ _____	_____	_____
8. _____	$ _____	_____	_____
9. _____	$ _____	_____	_____
10. _____	$ _____	_____	_____
11. _____	$ _____	_____	_____
12. _____	$ _____	_____	_____
13. _____	$ _____	_____	_____
14. _____	$ _____	_____	_____
15. _____	$ _____	_____	_____
16. _____	$ _____	_____	_____
17. _____	$ _____	_____	_____
18. _____	$ _____	_____	_____
19. _____	$ _____	_____	_____
20. _____	$ _____	_____	_____
21. _____	$ _____	_____	_____
22. _____	$ _____	_____	_____
23. _____	$ _____	_____	_____
24. _____	$ _____	_____	_____

Form G102

HOLIDAY MAILING LIST

Name:_____ Year:_____

Gift/Card Recipient	Address	Date Sent

HOUSEHOLD CHORES AND PROJECTS

Item To Be Done:	Assigned To:	Date Assigned:	Date Finished:

Form H103

INVENTORY OF COLLECTIBLES

Name: _____

Item	Purchase Date	Purchase Price	Estimated Value
_____	_____	$ _____	$ _____
_____	_____	$ _____	$ _____
_____	_____	$ _____	$ _____
_____	_____	$ _____	$ _____
_____	_____	$ _____	$ _____
_____	_____	$ _____	$ _____
_____	_____	$ _____	$ _____
_____	_____	$ _____	$ _____
_____	_____	$ _____	$ _____
_____	_____	$ _____	$ _____
_____	_____	$ _____	$ _____
_____	_____	$ _____	$ _____
_____	_____	$ _____	$ _____
_____	_____	$ _____	$ _____
_____	_____	$ _____	$ _____
_____	_____	$ _____	$ _____
_____	_____	$ _____	$ _____
_____	_____	$ _____	$ _____
_____	_____	$ _____	$ _____
_____	_____	$ _____	$ _____
_____	_____	$ _____	$ _____

Total: $ _____ $ _____

ITEMS TO BE RETURNED

Item Lent	Borrower	Date Lent	Date Returned	Returned Condition

ITEMS TO RETURN

Item Borrowed	Lender	Date Borrowed	Date Returned	Returned Condition
_____	_____	_____	_____	_____
_____	_____	_____	_____	_____
_____	_____	_____	_____	_____
_____	_____	_____	_____	_____
_____	_____	_____	_____	_____
_____	_____	_____	_____	_____
_____	_____	_____	_____	_____
_____	_____	_____	_____	_____
_____	_____	_____	_____	_____
_____	_____	_____	_____	_____
_____	_____	_____	_____	_____
_____	_____	_____	_____	_____
_____	_____	_____	_____	_____
_____	_____	_____	_____	_____
_____	_____	_____	_____	_____
_____	_____	_____	_____	_____
_____	_____	_____	_____	_____
_____	_____	_____	_____	_____
_____	_____	_____	_____	_____
_____	_____	_____	_____	_____
_____	_____	_____	_____	_____

MARRIAGE RECORDS

Husband's Full Name: _____

Wife's Full Name: _____

Marriage Date: _____ Officiated by: _____

Marriage Location: _____

     City: _____ County: _____ State: _____

Location of Marriage License or Certificate:_____

_____

Additional Information:_____

_____

_____

_____

If Re-Married:

Husband's Full Name: _____

Wife's Full Name: _____

Marriage Date: _____ Officiated by: _____

Marriage Location: _____

     City: _____ County: _____ State: _____

Location of Marriage License or Certificate:_____

_____

Additional Information:_____

_____

_____

_____

Form M101

OUTSTANDING BILLS RECORD

Name:_____ Date: _____

Pay To	Date Due	Amount Due	Date Paid	Amount Paid
_____	_____	$ _____	_____	$ _____
_____	_____	$ _____	_____	$ _____
_____	_____	$ _____	_____	$ _____
_____	_____	$ _____	_____	$ _____
_____	_____	$ _____	_____	$ _____
_____	_____	$ _____	_____	$ _____
_____	_____	$ _____	_____	$ _____
_____	_____	$ _____	_____	$ _____
_____	_____	$ _____	_____	$ _____
_____	_____	$ _____	_____	$ _____
_____	_____	$ _____	_____	$ _____
_____	_____	$ _____	_____	$ _____
_____	_____	$ _____	_____	$ _____
_____	_____	$ _____	_____	$ _____
_____	_____	$ _____	_____	$ _____
_____	_____	$ _____	_____	$ _____
_____	_____	$ _____	_____	$ _____
_____	_____	$ _____	_____	$ _____
_____	_____	$ _____	_____	$ _____
_____	_____	$ _____	_____	$ _____
_____	_____	$ _____	_____	$ _____
_____	_____	$ _____	_____	$ _____
_____	_____	$ _____	_____	$ _____

PERSONAL FACT SHEET

Name: _____ Birthdate: _____

Birthplace/City: _____ County: _____ State: _____

Social Security #: _____ Blood Type: _____

Driver's License #: _____ State Issued: _____

Location of Birth Certificate: _____

Other Identification: _____ Number: _____

Important Significant Events:

Event   Date

_____   _____

_____   _____

_____   _____

_____   _____

Location of Important Documents:

Name of Document   Location of Document

_____   _____

_____   _____

_____   _____

Marriage Date: _____ Name of Spouse: _____

City: _____ County: _____ State: _____

Birthdate of Spouse: _____ Birthplace: _____

Names of Children   Birthdates   Birthplaces of Children

_____   _____   _____

_____   _____   _____

_____   _____   _____

Other Information: _____

_____

PERSONAL INFORMATION SHEET

Date: _____

Full Legal Name: _____

Also Known As: _____

Date of Birth: _____ Place of Birth: _____

Country of Citizenship: _____

If Naturalized, Date of Naturalization: _____

Place of Naturalization: _____

If Resident Alien, Alien Registration #: _____

Social Security #: _____

Address: _____

Home Phone: _____ Work Phone: _____

Employer: _____

Employer Address _____

Bank Account #: _____ Bank Name: _____

Driver's License #: _____ State: _____ Expires: _____

Health Insurance: _____ Policy #: _____

Medical Insurance: _____ Policy #: _____

Dental Insurance: _____ Policy #: _____

Allergies: _____

Medical Problems: _____

Blood Type: _____ Organ Donor: (Yes) _____ (No) _____

If Veteran, Branch of Service, Unit: _____

Rank or Rate at Discharge: _____ Date Discharged: _____

In Case of an Emergency, Please Contact

Name: _____ Phone: _____

Relation: _____

PET CARE REGISTRY

Date of Visit:_____

Pet's Name: _____ Age: _____

Breed: _____ Color(s): _____

Name of Veterinarian:_____

Name of Clinic/Animal Hospital: _____

Location: _____ Phone: _____

Reason: _____

Diagnosis: _____

Treatment: _____

Cost: $ _____

Next Appointment Scheduled: _____ Time: _____

Reason: _____

_____

Date of Visit:_____

Pet's Name: _____ Age: _____

Breed: _____ Color(s): _____

Name of Veterinarian:_____

Name of Clinic/Animal Hospital: _____

Location: _____ Phone: _____

Reason: _____

Diagnosis: _____

Treatment: _____

Cost: $ _____

Next Appointment Scheduled: _____ Time: _____

Reason: _____

_____

REBATE RECEIPT LOG

Date Mailed	Manufacturer	Rebate Amount	Date Received
_____	_____	$ _____	_____
_____	_____	$ _____	_____
_____	_____	$ _____	_____
_____	_____	$ _____	_____
_____	_____	$ _____	_____
_____	_____	$ _____	_____
_____	_____	$ _____	_____
_____	_____	$ _____	_____
_____	_____	$ _____	_____
_____	_____	$ _____	_____
_____	_____	$ _____	_____
_____	_____	$ _____	_____
_____	_____	$ _____	_____
_____	_____	$ _____	_____
_____	_____	$ _____	_____
_____	_____	$ _____	_____
_____	_____	$ _____	

RECORD OF ACCIDENT CLAIMS

Name: _____

Claim Filed Against: _____ Filing Date:_____

Date of Accident:_____ Location: _____

Description of Claim: _____

_____

_____

Court: _____ Case #: _____ Phone: _____

Attorney: _____ Phone: _____

Other Information: _____

_____

_____

_____

Name: _____

Claim Filed Against: _____ Filing Date:_____

Date of Accident:_____ Location: _____

Description of Claim: _____

_____

_____

Court: _____ Case #: _____ Phone: _____

Attorney: _____ Phone: _____

Other Information: _____

_____

_____

_____

Form R101

RESIDENTIAL SERVICES SCHEDULE

Name: _____

Name of Company: _____ Date: _____
Service Required: _____
Amount Charged: $ _____ Amount Paid: $ _____ Balance: $_____

Name of Company: _____ Date: _____
Service Required: _____
Amount Charged: $ _____ Amount Paid: $ _____ Balance: $_____

Name of Company: _____ Date: _____
Service Required: _____
Amount Charged: $ _____ Amount Paid: $ _____ Balance: $_____

Name of Company: _____ Date: _____
Service Required: _____
Amount Charged: $ _____ Amount Paid: $ _____ Balance: $_____

Name of Company: _____ Date: _____
Service Required: _____
Amount Charged: $ _____ Amount Paid: $ _____ Balance: $_____

Name of Company: _____ Date: _____
Service Required: _____
Amount Charged: $ _____ Amount Paid: $ _____ Balance: $_____

SALE CALENDAR

Item	Sale Date	Discount	Sale Location
1. _____	_____	$ _____	_____
2. _____	_____	$ _____	_____
3. _____	_____	$ _____	_____
4. _____	_____	$ _____	_____
5. _____	_____	$ _____	_____
6. _____	_____	$ _____	_____
7. _____	_____	$ _____	_____
8. _____	_____	$ _____	_____
9. _____	_____	$ _____	_____
10. _____	_____	$ _____	_____
11. _____	_____	$ _____	_____
12. _____	_____	$ _____	_____
13. _____	_____	$ _____	_____
14. _____	_____	$ _____	_____
15. _____	_____	$ _____	_____
16. _____	_____	$ _____	_____
17. _____	_____	$ _____	_____
18. _____	_____	$ _____	_____
19. _____	_____	$ _____	_____
20. _____	_____	$ _____	_____
21. _____	_____	$ _____	_____
22. _____	_____	$ _____	_____
23. _____	_____	$ _____	_____
24. _____	_____	$ _____	_____
25. _____	_____	$ _____	_____

Form S106

TO DO TODAY

Name:_____ Day:_____ Date: _____

Appointments   Time

_____   _____

_____   _____

_____   _____

_____   _____

Tasks to be Completed   (✓) if Done

_____   _____

_____   _____

_____   _____

_____   _____

Calls to Make   Phone

_____   _____

_____   _____

_____   _____

_____   _____

Errands to Run

_____   _____

_____   _____

_____   _____

Other Information: _____

_____

TRAFFIC VIOLATIONS RECORD

Name:_____ Date: _____

Tickets Received

Ticket #: _____ Description: _____

Date: _____ Cost: $ _____ Points: _____

Ticket #: _____ Description: _____

Date: _____ Cost: $ _____ Points: _____

Ticket #: _____ Description: _____

Date: _____ Cost: $ _____ Points: _____

Ticket #: _____ Description: _____

Date: _____ Cost: $ _____ Points: _____

Total Points: _____

Defensive Driving Courses Taken:
Reason   Date

_____   _____

_____   _____

_____   _____

License Suspension/Revocation:
Reason   Date Began   Date Ended

_____   _____   _____

_____   _____   _____

_____   _____   _____

Additional Traffic-Related Charges: _____

_____

Additional Information:_____

_____

VEHICLE INSURANCE REGISTER

Vehicle Information

Title Holder: _____ Date: _____

License Plate #: _____ ID #: _____ State: _____

Make of Vehicle: _____ Model: _____ Year: _____

Registration #: _____ Expiration Date: _____

Insurance Information

Insurance Company: _____

Policy #: _____ Deductible Amount: $ _____

Liability Amount: _____

Other Coverages: _____

Annual Premium: _____ Due Date(s): _____

Agent's Name: _____

Address of Agent: _____

Agent's Phone: _____ Service/Claims Phone: _____

Policy Location: _____

Miscellaneous Details: _____

_____

_____

_____

_____

_____

_____

_____

VEHICLE REGISTRATION RECORD

Vehicle Owner:_____

Vehicle Description: _____

License Plate #:_____ State: _____

Registration Year: _____

Registration Renewal Fee: _____ Date Due: _____

Vehicle Owner:_____

Vehicle Description: _____

License Plate # _____ State: _____

Registration Year: _____

Registration Renewal Fee: _____ Date Due: _____

Vehicle Owner:_____

Vehicle Description: _____

License Plate #:_____ State: _____

Registration Year: _____

Registration Renewal Fee: _____ Date Due: _____

Vehicle Owner:_____

Vehicle Description: _____

License Plate #:_____ State: _____

Registration Year: _____

Registration Renewal Fee: _____ Date Due: _____

VOLUNTEER RECORD

Name: _____

Place Volunteered: _____

Location: _____ Phone: _____

Duties: _____

_____

Supervisor: _____

Dates Worked   Hours Worked

_____   _____

_____   _____

_____   _____

_____   _____

_____   _____

_____   _____

_____   _____

_____   _____

Total Volunteer Hours: _____

Comments: _____

_____

_____

_____

_____

_____

VOTING RECORD

Name: _____

Election Date: _____ Voting Location: _____

Public Office Position: _____

Candidates: _____ _____

_____ _____

_____ _____

Candidate Voted For: _____

Party Voted For: _____

Election Results: _____

Election Date: _____ Voting Location: _____

Public Office Position: _____

Candidates: _____ _____

_____ _____

_____ _____

Candidate Voted For: _____

Party Voted For: _____

Election Results: _____

Election Date: _____ Voting Location: _____

Public Office Position: _____

Candidates: _____ _____

_____ _____

_____ _____

_____ _____

Candidate Voted For: _____

Party Voted For: _____

Election Results: _____

Business forms

Section 2
Business forms

Forms in this section

ADVERTISING BUDGET

For The Year: _____

Company Name: _____

Month	Radio	Television	Newspaper	Other	Monthly Cost
January:	_____	_____	_____	_____	_____
February:	_____	_____	_____	_____	_____
March:	_____	_____	_____	_____	_____
April:	_____	_____	_____	_____	_____
May:	_____	_____	_____	_____	_____
June:	_____	_____	_____	_____	_____
July:	_____	_____	_____	_____	_____
August:	_____	_____	_____	_____	_____
September:	_____	_____	_____	_____	_____
October:	_____	_____	_____	_____	_____
November:	_____	_____	_____	_____	_____
December:	_____	_____	_____	_____	_____

Total Yearly Advertising Cost: $ _____

Form A201

ADVERTISING DIRECTORY

Medium: _____

Station/Publication Name: _____

Contact Person: _____

Advertising Contract: From: _____ To: _____

Rate:_____

Billing Address: _____

Phone: _____

Medium: _____

Station/Publication Name: _____

Contact Person: _____

Advertising Contract: From: _____ To: _____

Rate: _____

Billing Address: _____

Phone: _____

Medium: _____

Station/Publication Name: _____

Contact Person: _____

Advertising Contract: From: _____ To: _____

Rate: _____

Billing Address: _____

Phone: _____

ADVERTISING RECORD

Item Advertised	Date(s) Ad Aired/ Published	Advertising Medium	Number of Respondents	Sales Results
_____	_____	_____	_____	_____
_____	_____	_____	_____	_____
_____	_____	_____	_____	_____
_____	_____	_____	_____	_____
_____	_____	_____	_____	_____
_____	_____	_____	_____	_____
_____	_____	_____	_____	_____
_____	_____	_____	_____	_____
_____	_____	_____	_____	_____
_____	_____	_____	_____	_____
_____	_____	_____	_____	_____
_____	_____	_____	_____	_____
_____	_____	_____	_____	_____
_____	_____	_____	_____	_____
_____	_____	_____	_____	_____
_____	_____	_____	_____	_____
_____	_____	_____	_____	_____
_____	_____	_____	_____	_____
_____	_____	_____	_____	_____
_____	_____	_____	_____	_____
_____	_____	_____	_____	_____

Form A203

APPLICATIONS PENDING

Name: _____

Applied to: _____ Date: _____
Address: _____
Contact Name: _____ Phone: _____
Date of Follow-Up Contact: _____
Response: _____
_____

Applied to: _____ Date: _____
Address: _____
Contact Name: _____ Phone: _____
Date of Follow-Up Contact: _____
Response: _____
_____

Applied to: _____ Date: _____
Address: _____
Contact Name: _____ Phone: _____
Date of Follow-Up Contact: _____
Response: _____
_____

APPOINTMENTS

Name:_____Week of: _____

	Appointment with	Concerning	Phone	Time
Sunday:	_____	_____	_____	_____
	_____	_____	_____	_____
Monday:	_____	_____	_____	_____
	_____	_____	_____	_____
Tuesday:	_____	_____	_____	_____
	_____	_____	_____	_____
Wednesday:	_____	_____	_____	_____
	_____	_____	_____	_____
Thursday:	_____	_____	_____	_____
	_____	_____	_____	_____
Friday:	_____	_____	_____	_____
	_____	_____	_____	_____
Saturday:	_____	_____	_____	_____
	_____	_____	_____	_____

Notes: _____

_____

Form A205

BUSINESS HOLDINGS REGISTER

Name of Owner:_____ Date: _____

Name of Business:_____

Location: _____

Ownership Interest %: _____

Amount Paid: $ _____ Present Value: $ _____

Evidence of Ownership:_____

_____

Name of Owner:_____ Date: _____

Name of Business:_____

Location: _____

Ownership Interest %: _____

Amount Paid: $ _____ Present Value: $ _____

Evidence of Ownership:_____

_____

Name of Owner:_____ Date: _____

Name of Business:_____

Location: _____

Ownership Interest %: _____

Amount Paid: $ _____ Present Value: $ _____

Evidence of Ownership:_____

_____

BUSINESS INSURANCE

Company Name: _____

Property Covered: _____

Property Description: _____

_____

Address: _____

_____

Insurance Provider: _____ Policy #: _____

Coverage

Main Building Amount: $ _____ Other Buildings: $ _____

Personal Liability: $ _____ Public Liability: $_____

Company Property: $_____ Deductibles: $_____

Premium: $_____ Premium Due: _____

Expires: _____

Additional Coverages: _____

_____

_____

Insurance Agent: _____ Phone: _____

Address: _____

Policyholder Service or Claims Phone: _____

Insurance Policy Location: _____

Property Inventory Location: _____

Additional Information: _____

_____

_____

_____

Form B202

BUSINESS CONTACTS

Name of Business Contact: _____

Company: _____

Person's Title: _____ Phone: _____

Met at: _____ Date: _____

Issues Discussed: _____

Additional Information: _____

_____

Name of Business Contact: _____

Company: _____

Person's Title: _____ Phone: _____

Met at: _____ Date: _____

Issues Discussed: _____

Additional Information: _____

_____

Name of Business Contact: _____

Company: _____

Person's Title: _____ Phone: _____

Met at: _____ Date: _____

Issues Discussed: _____

Additional Information: _____

_____

DAILY AUTO MILEAGE LEDGER

Name:_____ Year:_____

Date	Destination	Purpose	Miles	Other Costs
_____	_____	_____	_____	$_____
_____	_____	_____	_____	$_____
_____	_____	_____	_____	$_____
_____	_____	_____	_____	$_____
_____	_____	_____	_____	$_____
_____	_____	_____	_____	$_____
_____	_____	_____	_____	$_____
_____	_____	_____	_____	$_____
_____	_____	_____	_____	$_____
_____	_____	_____	_____	$_____
_____	_____	_____	_____	$_____
_____	_____	_____	_____	$_____
_____	_____	_____	_____	$_____
_____	_____	_____	_____	$_____
_____	_____	_____	_____	$_____
_____	_____	_____	_____	$_____
_____	_____	_____	_____	$_____
_____	_____	_____	_____	$_____
_____	_____	_____	_____	$_____
_____	_____	_____	_____	$_____

Total: $ _____ $_____

Form D201

DAILY EXPENSE RECORD

Name:_____   Date:_____

Destination: Purpose: Miles Traveled:

_____   _____   _____

_____   _____   _____

_____   _____   _____

_____   _____   _____

Total Miles: _____   Breakfast: _____

Gas: _____   Lunch: _____

Tolls: _____   Dinner: _____

Parking: _____   Other Food: _____

Air Fare: _____   _____

Cab Fare: _____   Entertainment:

Car Rental: _____   _____

Other Travel: _____   Supplies: _____

Hotel: _____   Other: _____

Fees/Tips: _____   _____

Phone/Fax: _____   _____

TOTAL CHARGES: _____

SUBMITTED ON: _____

APPROVED: _____

PAID OUT ON: _____

EMPLOYEE BENEFIT PACKAGE

Name of Insured: _____ Insurance #:_____

Name of Employer:_____

Insurance Provider:_____

Company Contact: _____ Phone: _____

Benefit Plan Location:_____

Other Plan Information: _____

_____

Benefit Plan Effective Date: _____

List of Benefits Available:

Stock Options	$ _____
Restricted Stock	$ _____
Group Life Insurance	$ _____
Deferred Compensation	$ _____
Vested Employer's Contribution	$ _____
Savings Plan Contribution	$ _____
Vested Employee's Contribution	$ _____
Profit Sharing Plan Contribution	$ _____
Pension Plan Contribution	$ _____
Post-Death Salary Compensation	$ _____
Other	
_____	$ _____
_____	$ _____
_____	$ _____

HOME OFFICE PRODUCT ORDER FORM

Name: _____

Product	Date Ordered	Vendor	Quantity	Price
_____	_____	_____	_____	$ _____
_____	_____	_____	_____	$ _____
_____	_____	_____	_____	$ _____
_____	_____	_____	_____	$ _____
_____	_____	_____	_____	$ _____
_____	_____	_____	_____	$ _____
_____	_____	_____	_____	$ _____
_____	_____	_____	_____	$ _____
_____	_____	_____	_____	$ _____
_____	_____	_____	_____	$ _____
_____	_____	_____	_____	$ _____
_____	_____	_____	_____	$ _____
_____	_____	_____	_____	$ _____
_____	_____	_____	_____	$ _____
_____	_____	_____	_____	$ _____
_____	_____	_____	_____	$ _____
_____	_____	_____	_____	$ _____
_____	_____	_____	_____	$ _____
_____	_____	_____	_____	$ _____
_____	_____	_____	_____	$ _____
_____	_____	_____	_____	$ _____
_____	_____	_____	_____	$ _____

Total Price: $ _____

HOURLY WORK SCHEDULE

Name: _____

Employer: _____

Location: _____

Salary/Hr.: _____

Hours Worked:

Week of:	Sun.	Mon.	Tue.	Wed.	Thur.	Fri.	Sat.	Total Hours	Total Pay	Date Paid
	___	___	___	___	___	___	___	___	___	___
	___	___	___	___	___	___	___	___	___	___
	___	___	___	___	___	___	___	___	___	___
	___	___	___	___	___	___	___	___	___	___
	___	___	___	___	___	___	___	___	___	___
	___	___	___	___	___	___	___	___	___	___
	___	___	___	___	___	___	___	___	___	___
	___	___	___	___	___	___	___	___	___	___
	___	___	___	___	___	___	___	___	___	___
	___	___	___	___	___	___	___	___	___	___
	___	___	___	___	___	___	___	___	___	___
	___	___	___	___	___	___	___	___	___	___
	___	___	___	___	___	___	___	___	___	___
	___	___	___	___	___	___	___	___	___	___
	___	___	___	___	___	___	___	___	___	___
	___	___	___	___	___	___	___	___	___	___
	___	___	___	___	___	___	___	___	___	___

Form H202

JOB APPLICANT RATING

Applicant:_____

Position: _____

Department: _____

Use the following scale to rate applicant's qualifications:

        5) Excellent   2) Below Average
        4) Above Average   1) Unacceptable
        3) Fully Qualified   0) Unobserved

Education   _____

Experience   _____

Attention to Detail   _____

Cooperation   _____

Initiative   _____

Integrity   _____

Interpersonal Skills   _____

Learning Ability   _____

Stress Tolerance   _____

Verbal Communication   _____

Overall:

_____Exceptional   _____Strong   _____Acceptable

_____Weak   _____Totally unacceptable

Recommendation:

_____Hire

_____Reject

_____Other _____

Signed:

_____   _____
Interviewer   Date

JOB ESTIMATES

Project: _____

_____

Contractor: _____

Address: _____

Phone: _____ Bid: _____

Start Date: _____ Project Completion Date: _____

Additional Information: _____

_____

Contractor: _____

Address: _____

Phone: _____ Bid: _____

Start Date: _____ Project Completion Date: _____

Additional Information: _____

_____

Contractor: _____

Address: _____

Phone: _____ Bid: _____

Start Date: _____ Project Completion Date: _____

Additional Information: _____

_____

JOB HISTORY RECORD

Name: _____

Employer: _____

Address: _____

Type of Business/Organization: _____

Title/Position: _____ Hrs./Wk.: _____

Dates Employed: from _____ to _____

Starting Salary: $ _____ Ending Salary: $ _____

Job Responsibilities: _____

_____

Name of Supervisor: _____

Reason for Leaving: _____

Comments: _____

_____

Employer: _____

Address: _____

Type of Business/Organization: _____

Title/Position: _____ Hrs./Wk.: _____

Dates Employed: from _____ to _____

Starting Salary: $ _____ Ending Salary: $ _____

Job Responsibilities: _____

_____

Name of Supervisor: _____

Reason for Leaving: _____

Comments: _____

_____

LIMITED PARTNERSHIP LOG

Name of Partnership	Date Partnership Formed	Percent of Ownership Interest	General or Limited Partner	Amount of Investment
_____	_____	_____	_____	_____
_____	_____	_____	_____	_____
_____	_____	_____	_____	_____
_____	_____	_____	_____	_____
_____	_____	_____	_____	_____
_____	_____	_____	_____	_____
_____	_____	_____	_____	_____
_____	_____	_____	_____	_____
_____	_____	_____	_____	_____
_____	_____	_____	_____	_____
_____	_____	_____	_____	_____
_____	_____	_____	_____	_____
_____	_____	_____	_____	_____
_____	_____	_____	_____	_____
_____	_____	_____	_____	_____
_____	_____	_____	_____	_____
_____	_____	_____	_____	_____
_____	_____	_____	_____	_____
_____	_____	_____	_____	_____
_____	_____	_____	_____	_____
_____	_____	_____	_____	_____
_____	_____	_____	_____	_____

LONG DISTANCE PHONE CALL RECORD

Date	Name of Caller	Party Called	Number Called	Time from - to

MEETING AGENDA

Organization: _____

Meeting Date: _____ Location: _____

Issues Pending	Action Taken
_____	_____
_____	_____
_____	_____
_____	_____
_____	_____
_____	_____
_____	_____
_____	_____

Additional Discussion: _____

_____

_____

_____

Persons Attending

_____	_____	_____
_____	_____	_____
_____	_____	_____
_____	_____	_____
_____	_____	_____
_____	_____	_____
_____	_____	_____

Form M201

MEETING SCHEDULE

Name: _____

Meeting with: _____ Date: _____

Time: _____ Location: _____

Contact Person: _____ Phone: _____

Name: _____

Meeting with: _____ Date: _____

Time: _____ Location: _____

Contact Person: _____ Phone: _____

Name: _____

Meeting with: _____ Date: _____

Time: _____ Location: _____

Contact Person: _____ Phone: _____

Name: _____

Meeting with: _____ Date: _____

Time: _____ Location: _____

Contact Person: _____ Phone: _____

Name: _____

Meeting with: _____ Date: _____

Time: _____ Location: _____

Contact Person: _____ Phone: _____

MONTHLY BALANCE SHEET

FOR THE MONTH OF: _____

PROFIT

	Total Sales for the Month:	_____
−	Cost of Goods Sold:	_____
=	**GROSS PROFIT:**	_____

EXPENSES

Operating Costs

Supplies	_____
Advertising	_____
Utilities	_____
Payroll	_____
Taxes	_____
Travel	_____
Other	_____

Fixed Costs

Rent	_____
Insurance	_____
Depreciation	_____
Other	_____

TOTAL EXPENSES: _____

	GROSS PROFIT:	_____
−	TOTAL EXPENSES:	_____
=	**TOTAL NET MONTHLY INCOME*:**	_____

*This total does not reflect taxes or distributions to be taken out.

OCCUPATIONAL LICENSE LISTING

Name: _____

License Title: _____

License #: _____

Purpose: _____

Issued by: _____

Date Issued:_____ Date Expires: _____

License Renewal Fee: _____

Additional Information:_____

License Title: _____

License #: _____

Purpose: _____

Issued by: _____

Date Issued:_____ Date Expires: _____

License Renewal Fee: _____

Additional Information:_____

License Title: _____

License #: _____

Purpose: _____

Issued by: _____

Date Issued:_____ Date Expires: _____

License Renewal Fee: _____

Additional Information:_____

PATENTS RECEIVED

Name: _____

Patent #: _____

Patent Description: _____

_____

Date Applied for: _____ Date Issued: _____

Patent Expiration Date: _____

Other Information: _____

Patent #: _____

Patent Description: _____

_____

Date Applied for: _____ Date Issued: _____

Patent Expiration Date: _____

Other Information: _____

Patent #: _____

Patent Description: _____

_____

Date Applied for: _____ Date Issued: _____

Patent Expiration Date: _____

Other Information: _____

Patent #: _____

Patent Description: _____

_____

Date Applied for: _____ Date Issued: _____

Patent Expiration Date: _____

Other Information: _____

PROPERTY AND LIABILITY INSURANCE COVERAGE

Name of Insured: _____

Property Covered: _____

Property Description: _____

_____

Address: _____

_____

Insurance Provider: _____ Policy #: _____

Coverage

Dwelling Amount: $ _____ Other Buildings: $ _____

Personal Property: $ _____ Living Expense: $_____

Personal Liability: $ _____ Public Liability: $_____

Deductibles: $ _____ Premium: $ _____

Premium Due: _____ Expires: _____

Additional Coverages: _____

_____

_____

Insurance Agent: _____ Phone: _____

Address: _____

Policyholder Service or Claims Phone: _____

Insurance Policy Location:_____

Property Inventory Location: _____

Additional Information:_____

_____

_____

_____

RECORD OF ATTENDANCE

Name: _____ Year: _____

Place of Attendance: _____

	Jan.	Feb.	Mar.	Apr.	May	June	July	Aug.	Sept.	Oct.	Nov.	Dec.
1	____	____	____	____	____	____	____	____	____	____	____	____
2	____	____	____	____	____	____	____	____	____	____	____	____
3	____	____	____	____	____	____	____	____	____	____	____	____
4	____	____	____	____	____	____	____	____	____	____	____	____
5	____	____	____	____	____	____	____	____	____	____	____	____
6	____	____	____	____	____	____	____	____	____	____	____	____
7	____	____	____	____	____	____	____	____	____	____	____	____
8	____	____	____	____	____	____	____	____	____	____	____	____
9	____	____	____	____	____	____	____	____	____	____	____	____
10	____	____	____	____	____	____	____	____	____	____	____	____
11	____	____	____	____	____	____	____	____	____	____	____	____
12	____	____	____	____	____	____	____	____	____	____	____	____
13	____	____	____	____	____	____	____	____	____	____	____	____
14	____	____	____	____	____	____	____	____	____	____	____	____
15	____	____	____	____	____	____	____	____	____	____	____	____
16	____	____	____	____	____	____	____	____	____	____	____	____
17	____	____	____	____	____	____	____	____	____	____	____	____
18	____	____	____	____	____	____	____	____	____	____	____	____
19	____	____	____	____	____	____	____	____	____	____	____	____
20	____	____	____	____	____	____	____	____	____	____	____	____
21	____	____	____	____	____	____	____	____	____	____	____	____
22	____	____	____	____	____	____	____	____	____	____	____	____
23	____	____	____	____	____	____	____	____	____	____	____	____
24	____	____	____	____	____	____	____	____	____	____	____	____
25	____	____	____	____	____	____	____	____	____	____	____	____
26	____	____	____	____	____	____	____	____	____	____	____	____
27	____	____	____	____	____	____	____	____	____	____	____	____
28	____	____	____	____	____	____	____	____	____	____	____	____
29	____	____	____	____	____	____	____	____	____	____	____	____
30	____	____	____	____	____	____	____	____	____	____	____	____
31	____	____	____	____	____	____	____	____	____	____	____	____
Total:	____	____	____	____	____	____	____	____	____	____	____	____

Form R201

RENTAL PROPERTY

Location of Property: _____

Description of Property: _____

_____

Tenants: _____ Phone: _____

Rental Date: from _____ to _____

Terms of Rental Agreement: _____

_____

_____

_____

Rent: _____ Due: _____

Other Information: _____

_____

Location of Property: _____

Description of Property: _____

_____

Tenants: _____ Phone: _____

Rental Date: from _____ to _____

Terms of Rental Agreement: _____

_____

_____

_____

Rent: _____ Due: _____

Other Information: _____

_____

SALES PROSPECTS

Date: _____

Name of Prospect/Business: _____

Address: _____

Contact: _____ Phone: _____ Date of Call: _____

Results: _____

Name of Prospect/Business: _____

Address: _____

Contact: _____ Phone: _____ Date of Call: _____

Results: _____

Name of Prospect/Business: _____

Address: _____

Contact: _____ Phone: _____ Date of Call: _____

Results: _____

Name of Prospect/Business: _____

Address: _____

Contact: _____ Phone: _____ Date of Call: _____

Results: _____

Name of Prospect/Business: _____

Address: _____

Contact: _____ Phone: _____ Date of Call: _____

Results: _____

Form S201

SALES RECORD

Name: _____

Name of Account	Account #	Date of Sale	Amount of Sale
_____	_____	_____	$ _____
_____	_____	_____	$ _____
_____	_____	_____	$ _____
_____	_____	_____	$ _____
_____	_____	_____	$ _____
_____	_____	_____	$ _____
_____	_____	_____	$ _____
_____	_____	_____	$ _____
_____	_____	_____	$ _____
_____	_____	_____	$ _____
_____	_____	_____	$ _____
_____	_____	_____	$ _____
_____	_____	_____	$ _____
_____	_____	_____	$ _____
_____	_____	_____	$ _____
_____	_____	_____	$ _____
_____	_____	_____	$ _____
_____	_____	_____	$ _____
_____	_____	_____	$ _____
_____	_____	_____	$ _____
_____	_____	_____	$ _____
_____	_____	_____	$ _____

Total Sales: $ _____

SCHEDULE OF BUSINESS TRIPS

Traveler's Name: _____ Date: _____

Destination: _____

Date of Arrival: _____ Time: _____

Date of Return: _____ Time: _____

Appointment with: _____ Position: _____

Company: _____ Phone: _____

Address: _____

Date:_____ from: _____ to: _____

Topic of Meeting:_____

Appointment with: _____ Position: _____

Company: _____ Phone: _____

Address: _____

Date:_____ from: _____ to: _____

Topic of Meeting:_____

Appointment with: _____ Position: _____

Company: _____ Phone: _____

Address: _____

Date:_____ from: _____ to: _____

Topic of Meeting:_____

Appointment with:_____ Position: _____

Company: _____ Phone: _____

Address: _____

Date:_____ from: _____ to: _____

Topic of Meeting:_____

Form S203

SOFTWARE AND COMPUTER INVENTORY

ID #	Name/Title	Computer	Location	Version

UTILITIES COST INVENTORY

Name: _____

Utility	Billing Date	Cost This Month	Cost Last Month
_____	_____	$_____	$_____
_____	_____	$_____	$_____
_____	_____	$_____	$_____
_____	_____	$_____	$_____
_____	_____	$_____	$_____
_____	_____	$_____	$_____
_____	_____	$_____	$_____
_____	_____	$_____	$_____
_____	_____	$_____	$_____
_____	_____	$_____	$_____
_____	_____	$_____	$_____
_____	_____	$_____	$_____
_____	_____	$_____	$_____
_____	_____	$_____	$_____
_____	_____	$_____	$_____
_____	_____	$_____	$_____
_____	_____	$_____	$_____
_____	_____	$_____	$_____
_____	_____	$_____	$_____
_____	_____	$_____	$_____
_____	_____	$_____	$_____
	Total:	$_____	$_____

Form U201

Educational records

Section 3
Educational records

Forms in this section

COURSE ASSIGNMENTS

Name of Student: _____ Week of: _____

Course: _____

Assignment: _____

Supplies/Materials Needed: _____

_____

Preparation Methods: _____

_____

Additional Information: _____

_____

Estimated Completion Time: _____

Date Assigned: _____ Due Date: _____ Time Due: _____

Course: _____

Assignment: _____

Supplies/Materials Needed: _____

_____

Preparation Methods: _____

_____

Additional Information: _____

_____

Estimated Completion Time: _____

Date Assigned: _____ Due Date: _____ Time Due: _____

Form C301

CURRICULUM

Name of Student: _____ Date: _____

School: _____

	Class/Instructor	Hours	Room
Monday:	_____	_____ to _____	_____
	_____	_____ to _____	_____
	_____	_____ to _____	_____
	_____	_____ to _____	_____
Tuesday:	_____	_____ to _____	_____
	_____	_____ to _____	_____
	_____	_____ to _____	_____
	_____	_____ to _____	_____
Wednesday:	_____	_____ to _____	_____
	_____	_____ to _____	_____
	_____	_____ to _____	_____
	_____	_____ to _____	_____
Thursday:	_____	_____ to _____	_____
	_____	_____ to _____	_____
	_____	_____ to _____	_____
	_____	_____ to _____	_____
Friday:	_____	_____ to _____	_____
	_____	_____ to _____	_____
	_____	_____ to _____	_____
	_____	_____ to _____	_____
Saturday:	_____	_____ to _____	_____
	_____	_____ to _____	_____
	_____	_____ to _____	_____
	_____	_____ to _____	_____

GRADE SCHOOL RECORD

Name of Student: _____

School Attended: _____

Location: _____ Phone: _____

Dates Attended: _____ to _____ Grades Completed: _____

Graduation Date: _____ Grade Point Average: _____

Activities: _____

Honors/Awards: _____

Other Information: _____

_____

School Attended: _____

Location: _____ Phone: _____

Dates Attended: _____ to _____ Grades Completed: _____

Graduation Date: _____ Grade Point Average: _____

Activities: _____

Honors/Awards: _____

Other Information: _____

_____

School Attended: _____

Location: _____ Phone: _____

Dates Attended: _____ to _____ Grades Completed: _____

Graduation Date: _____ Grade Point Average: _____

Activities: _____

Honors/Awards: _____

Other Information: _____

_____

HIGH SCHOOL RECORD

Name of Student: _____

School Attended: _____

Location: _____ Phone: _____

Dates Attended: _____ to _____ Grades Completed: _____

Graduation Date: _____ Overall Grade Point Average: _____

Clubs/Activities: _____

_____

_____

Sports Participated In: _____

_____

Honors/Awards: _____

_____

_____

Advanced Placement (AP) Courses:

Course	Date Taken	AP Test Grade	College Credit
_____	_____to_____	_____	_____
_____	_____to_____	_____	_____
_____	_____to_____	_____	_____
_____	_____to_____	_____	_____

PSAT:

Date Taken: _____ Score Received: _____

SAT:

Date Taken: _____ Score Received: _____

Practical Skills/Experience Acquired: _____

_____

MILITARY SERVICE RECORD

Name: _____

Branch of Service:_____ Service #: _____

Selective Service Registration Date: _____

Date of Valid Department of Defense Form DD-214: _____

Years of Service:_____ Date Completed Service:_____

Type of Discharge:_____

Military Occupation Specialty, Number and Title: _____

_____

Beginning Rate/Rank:_____ Date: _____

Promotions	Date	Additional Responsibilities
_____	_____	_____
_____	_____	_____
_____	_____	_____
_____	_____	_____

Medals, Awards Received:_____

_____

Military Programs Involved In: _____

_____

Special Training/Skills: _____

_____

Official Military Benefits: _____

_____

_____

Other Information: _____

_____

Form M301

PERSONAL REPORT CARD

Name: _____

Course: _____ Credits: _____ Instructor: _____

Course Taken at: _____ Date: _____ to _____

Grades:

Homework _____ _____ _____ _____ _____ _____ _____ _____

_____ _____ _____ _____ _____ _____ _____ _____

_____ _____ _____ _____ _____ _____ _____ _____

_____ _____ _____ _____ _____ _____ _____ _____

Quizzes _____ _____ _____ _____ _____ _____ _____ _____

Exams _____ _____ _____ _____ _____ _____ _____ _____

Project _____ Points/Grade_____

Project _____ Points/Grade_____

Project _____ Points/Grade_____

Midterm Grade _____ Final Grade _____

Course: _____ Credits: _____ Instructor: _____

Course Taken at: _____ Date: _____ to _____

Grades:

Homework _____ _____ _____ _____ _____ _____ _____ _____

_____ _____ _____ _____ _____ _____ _____ _____

_____ _____ _____ _____ _____ _____ _____ _____

_____ _____ _____ _____ _____ _____ _____ _____

Quizzes _____ _____ _____ _____ _____ _____ _____ _____

Exams _____ _____ _____ _____ _____ _____ _____ _____

Project _____ Points/Grade_____

Project _____ Points/Grade_____

Project _____ Points/Grade_____

Midterm Grade _____ Final Grade _____

SCHOLASTIC COLLEGE RECORD

Name of Student: _____

Name of College/University: _____

School Address: _____ Phone: _____

Dates Attended: _____ to _____ Total Years: _____

Major: _____ Major GPA: _____

Minor: _____ Minor GPA: _____

Cumulative GPA: _____ Total Credits: _____

Degree(s) Earned: _____ Date: _____

_____ Date: _____

Tests:	Date Taken	Score	Percentile		Date Taken	Score	Percentile
CLAST	_____	_____	_____	GRE	_____	_____	_____
LSAT	_____	_____	_____	MCAT	_____	_____	_____

Honors/Awards/Scholarships: _____

_____

_____

Clubs/Activities: _____

_____

_____

Practical Experience/Skills Acquired: _____

_____

_____

Comments/Other Information: _____

_____

_____

_____

Form S301

SPECIAL COMMENDATIONS/AWARDS

Name of Award Recipient:_____

Award/Honor/Special Recognition Received: _____

_____ Date Received:_____

Accomplishment Honored: _____

_____

Other Relevant Information: _____

_____

_____

Name of Award Recipient:_____

Award/Honor/Special Recognition Received: _____

_____ Date Received:_____

Accomplishment Honored: _____

_____

Other Relevant Information: _____

_____

_____

Name of Award Recipient:_____

Award/Honor/Special Recognition Received: _____

_____ Date Received:_____

Accomplishment Honored: _____

_____

Other Relevant Information: _____

_____

STANDARDIZED TEST SCORES

Name:_____ Age: _____

Test: _____ Score: _____ Percentile:_____

Date Taken:_____ Test Location: _____

Purpose of Test: _____

Retest Score, if Applicable: _____ Retest Date: _____

Deadline to Reapply for Next Testing: _____

Test Cost: _____ Additional Fees: _____

Contact Person:_____ Phone: _____

Name:_____ Age: _____

Test: _____ Score: _____ Percentile:_____

Date Taken:_____ Test Location: _____

Purpose of Test: _____

Retest Score, if Applicable: _____ Retest Date: _____

Deadline to Reapply for Next Testing: _____

Test Cost: _____ Additional Fees: _____

Contact Person:_____ Phone: _____

Name:_____ Age: _____

Test: _____ Score: _____ Percentile:_____

Date Taken:_____ Test Location: _____

Purpose of Test: _____

Retest Score, if Applicable: _____ Retest Date: _____

Deadline to Reapply for Next Testing: _____

Test Cost: _____ Additional Fees: _____

Contact Person:_____ Phone: _____

Form S303

VOCATIONAL / PROFESSIONAL TRAINING

Name: _____

Name of School/Training Center: _____

Address:_____ Phone: _____

Training Dates: _____ to_____ Total Training Hours: _____

Purpose: _____

Skills/Equipment Learned: _____

Company Sponsor (if applicable): _____

Certificates/Awards Received: _____

Name of School/Training Center: _____

Address:_____ Phone: _____

Training Dates: _____ to_____ Total Training Hours: _____

Purpose: _____

Skills/Equipment Learned: _____

Company Sponsor (if applicable): _____

Certificates/Awards Received: _____

Name of School/Training Center: _____

Address:_____ Phone: _____

Training Dates: _____ to_____ Total Training Hours: _____

Purpose: _____

Skills/Equipment Learned: _____

Company Sponsor (if applicable): _____

Certificates/Awards Received: _____

Health records

Section 4
Health records

Forms in this section

CHART OF CHILD'S GROWTH

Name of Child: _____ Date of Birth: _____

Date	Age	Height	Weight	Comments
_____	_____	_____	_____	_____
_____	_____	_____	_____	_____
_____	_____	_____	_____	_____
_____	_____	_____	_____	_____
_____	_____	_____	_____	_____
_____	_____	_____	_____	_____
_____	_____	_____	_____	_____
_____	_____	_____	_____	_____
_____	_____	_____	_____	_____
_____	_____	_____	_____	_____
_____	_____	_____	_____	_____
_____	_____	_____	_____	_____
_____	_____	_____	_____	_____
_____	_____	_____	_____	_____
_____	_____	_____	_____	_____
_____	_____	_____	_____	_____
_____	_____	_____	_____	_____
_____	_____	_____	_____	_____
_____	_____	_____	_____	_____
_____	_____	_____	_____	_____

DAILY DIET LOG

Name of Calorie Counter: _____

Day: _____ Date: _____ Weight: _____

	Menu	Calories	Fat
Breakfast:	_____	_____	_____
	_____	_____	_____
	_____	_____	_____
	_____	_____	_____
Lunch:	_____	_____	_____
	_____	_____	_____
	_____	_____	_____
	_____	_____	_____
	_____	_____	_____
Dinner:	_____	_____	_____
	_____	_____	_____
	_____	_____	_____
	_____	_____	_____
	_____	_____	_____
Snacks:	_____	_____	_____
	_____	_____	_____
	_____	_____	_____

Total Calories Consumed: _____   Total Fat Consumed: _____

Total Calories Allowed: _____   Total Fat Allowed: _____

Net +/-: _____   Net +/-: _____

Form D403

DENTAL VISIT LOG

Name of Patient:_____ Year: _____

Dentist:_____ Phone:_____

Address: _____

Orthodontist:_____ Phone:_____

Address: _____

Date	Reason for Visit/Treatment	Cost
_____	_____	$ _____
_____	_____	$ _____
_____	_____	$ _____
_____	_____	$ _____
_____	_____	$ _____
_____	_____	$ _____
_____	_____	$ _____
_____	_____	$ _____
_____	_____	$ _____
_____	_____	$ _____
_____	_____	$ _____
_____	_____	$ _____
_____	_____	$ _____
_____	_____	$ _____
_____	_____	$ _____
_____	_____	$ _____
_____	_____	$ _____
_____	_____	$ _____

Total Annual Dental Cost $ _____

DIET/FITNESS PROGRESS CHART

WEEK OF: _____

Beginning Weight: _____

Beginning Measurements: Chest_____   Waist _____

                                  Hips _____   Thighs _____

	Calories Consumed:	Exercise:	Weight
MONDAY:	_____	_____	_____
Notes:			
TUESDAY:	_____	_____	_____
Notes:			
WEDNESDAY:	_____	_____	_____
Notes:			
THURSDAY:	_____	_____	_____
Notes:			
FRIDAY:	_____	_____	_____
Notes:			
SATURDAY:	_____	_____	_____
Notes:			
SUNDAY:	_____	_____	_____
Notes:			

Ending Weight: _____

Ending Measurements: Chest _____   Waist _____

                              Hips _____   Thighs _____

Form D404

FITNESS TRAINING SCHEDULE

Name: _____

Name of Fitness Center: _____ Phone: _____

Sunday   (-   -   )

Workout Planned: _____

Workout Completed: _____

Monday   (-   -   )

Workout Planned: _____

Workout Completed: _____

Tuesday   (-   -   )

Workout Planned: _____

Workout Completed: _____

Wednesday   (-   -   )

Workout Planned: _____

Workout Completed: _____

Thursday   (-   -   )

Workout Planned: _____

Workout Completed: _____

Friday   (-   -   )

Workout Planned: _____

Workout Completed: _____

Saturday   (-   -   )

Workout Planned: _____

Workout Completed: _____

HEALTH INSURANCE

Name of Insured: _____ Date: _____

Insurance Company: _____

Policy #:_____ Premium: $ _____ per _____

Premium Due: _____ Type of Policy: _____

Agent: _____

Address: _____

Phone: _____ Location of Policy: _____

_____

Secondary Coverage: _____

_____

_____

_____

Terms of Contract: _____

_____

_____

_____

_____

Exceptions: _____

_____

_____

_____

Additional Information: _____

_____

_____

_____

_____

HOSPITALIZATION RECORD

Name: _____

Dates of Hospitalization: _____ to _____

Name of Hospital: _____ Phone: _____

Location: _____

Condition: _____

_____

Treatment: _____

Hospitalization Costs: _____

Attending Physician: _____

Comments: _____

_____

Name: _____

Dates of Hospitalization: _____ to _____

Name of Hospital: _____ Phone: _____

Location: _____

Condition: _____

_____

Treatment: _____

Hospitalization Costs: _____

Attending Physician: _____

Comments: _____

_____

LIFE INSURANCE FACT SHEET

Name of Insured: _____ Date: _____

Policy Holder: _____ Policy #:_____

Name of Insurance Company: _____

Agent:_____ Type of Policy: _____

Address:_____ Phone : _____

Anniversary Date of Policy: _____

Location of Policy: _____

Primary Beneficiary: _____

Secondary Beneficiary: _____

Face: $ _____ Premium: $_____ per _____

Other Important Information:_____

_____

_____

_____

_____

_____

_____

_____

_____

_____

_____

_____

_____

Form L401

LISTING OF MEDICAL SERVICES

Name: _____

Physician: _____ Phone: _____
    Address: _____

Gynecologist: _____ Phone: _____
    Address: _____

Optometrist: _____ Phone: _____
    Address: _____

Dentist:_____ Phone: _____
    Address: _____

Orthodontist:_____ Phone: _____
    Address: _____

Veterinarian_____ Phone: _____
    Address: _____

Hospital: _____ Phone: _____
    Address: _____

Pharmacy: _____ Phone: _____
    Address: _____

Other/Specialists: _____ Phone: _____
    Address: _____

Other/Specialists: _____ Phone: _____
    Address: _____

Other/Specialists: _____ Phone: _____
    Address: _____

MEDICAL EXPENSE LEDGER

Name:_____ Year:_____

Date	Service Provider	Cost	Third-Party Paid (✓)	Net Expense
_____	_____	$ _____	_____	$ _____
_____	_____	$ _____	_____	$ _____
_____	_____	$ _____	_____	$ _____
_____	_____	$ _____	_____	$ _____
_____	_____	$ _____	_____	$ _____
_____	_____	$ _____	_____	$ _____
_____	_____	$ _____	_____	$ _____
_____	_____	$ _____	_____	$ _____
_____	_____	$ _____	_____	$ _____
_____	_____	$ _____	_____	$ _____
_____	_____	$ _____	_____	$ _____
_____	_____	$ _____	_____	$ _____
_____	_____	$ _____	_____	$ _____
_____	_____	$ _____	_____	$ _____
	Annual Total:	$ _____		$ _____

Form M401

OPTICAL RECORD

Name:_____ Date: _____

Physician: _____ Phone : _____

Address: _____

Prescription:

	O.S.	O.D.

Sphere   _____ / _____

Cylinder   _____ / _____

Axis   _____ / _____

Add   _____ / _____

Comments/Information: _____

_____

_____

_____

Name:_____ Date: _____

Physician: _____ Phone : _____

Address: _____

Prescription:

	O.S.	O.D.

Sphere   _____ / _____

Cylinder   _____ / _____

Axis   _____ / _____

Add   _____ / _____

Comments/Information: _____

_____

_____

_____

PERSONAL HEALTH RECORD

Name: _____

Date: _____ Purpose of Visit/Symptoms:_____

_____

Treatment/Diagnosis:_____

_____

Physician: _____ Phone: _____

Date: _____ Purpose of Visit/Symptoms:_____

_____

Treatment/Diagnosis:_____

_____

Physician: _____ Phone: _____

Date: _____ Purpose of Visit/Symptoms:_____

_____

Treatment/Diagnosis:_____

_____

Physician: _____ Phone: _____

Prior Health Problems:_____

_____

_____

Allergies:_____

_____

_____

Family History of Disease:_____

_____

_____

Form P401

RECORDS OF BIRTH

Name: _____ Sex: _____

Parents' Names: _____

Birth Date: _____ Time of Birth: _____

Place of Birth: _____

Name of Hospital: _____ Phone: _____

Address: _____

Attending Physician: _____

Birthweight: _____ Length: _____

Hair Color: _____ Eye Color: _____ Blood Type: _____

Namesake: _____

Birthmarks/Distinguishing Traits: _____

_____

Relevant Information: _____

_____

_____

_____

_____

_____

_____

_____

_____

_____

_____

_____

_____

_____

REGISTRY OF PRESCRIPTIONS

Name: _____

Name of Drug: _____ Rx #: _____

Date Prescribed: _____ Exp. Date: _____

Physician: _____ Phone: _____

Pharmacy: _____ Phone: _____

Comments: _____

_____

_____

Name: _____

Name of Drug: _____ Rx #: _____

Date Prescribed: _____ Exp. Date: _____

Physician: _____ Phone: _____

Pharmacy: _____ Phone: _____

Comments: _____

_____

_____

Name: _____

Name of Drug: _____ Rx #: _____

Date Prescribed: _____ Exp. Date: _____

Physician: _____ Phone: _____

Pharmacy: _____ Phone: _____

Comments: _____

_____

_____

Form R402

ROUTINE CHECKUPS

Dental:

Patient Name	Date Last Checkup	Dentist	Next Checkup Due Date	Phone
_____	_____	_____	_____	_____
_____	_____	_____	_____	_____
_____	_____	_____	_____	_____
_____	_____	_____	_____	_____
_____	_____	_____	_____	_____
_____	_____	_____	_____	_____
_____	_____	_____	_____	_____
_____	_____	_____	_____	_____

Medical:

Patient Name	Date Last Checkup	Doctor	Next Checkup Due Date	Phone
_____	_____	_____	_____	_____
_____	_____	_____	_____	_____
_____	_____	_____	_____	_____
_____	_____	_____	_____	_____
_____	_____	_____	_____	_____
_____	_____	_____	_____	_____
_____	_____	_____	_____	_____

SCHEDULE OF VACCINATIONS

Name: _____

Vaccinated Against: _____ Date: _____

Name of Clinic and/or Physician: _____

Phone: _____ Booster/Revaccination Date: _____

Location of Stamped Certificate: _____

Other Information: _____

Name: _____

Vaccinated Against: _____ Date: _____

Name of Clinic and/or Physician: _____

Phone: _____ Booster/Revaccination Date: _____

Location of Stamped Certificate: _____

Other Information: _____

Name: _____

Vaccinated Against: _____ Date: _____

Name of Clinic and/or Physician: _____

Phone: _____ Booster/Revaccination Date: _____

Location of Stamped Certificate: _____

Other Information: _____

Name: _____

Vaccinated Against: _____ Date: _____

Name of Clinic and/or Physician: _____

Phone: _____ Booster/Revaccination Date: _____

Location of Stamped Certificate: _____

Other Information: _____

Form S401

WEIGHT TRACKING GUIDE

Name: _____

Date	Day	Weight	Comments
_____	_____	_____	_____
_____	_____	_____	_____
_____	_____	_____	_____
_____	_____	_____	_____
_____	_____	_____	_____
_____	_____	_____	_____
_____	_____	_____	_____
_____	_____	_____	_____
_____	_____	_____	_____
_____	_____	_____	_____
_____	_____	_____	_____
_____	_____	_____	_____
_____	_____	_____	_____
_____	_____	_____	_____
_____	_____	_____	_____
_____	_____	_____	_____
_____	_____	_____	_____
_____	_____	_____	_____
_____	_____	_____	_____
_____	_____	_____	_____
_____	_____	_____	_____

Investments/financial records

5

Section 5

Investments/ financial records

Forms in this section

ACCOUNTS RECEIVABLE

Name: _____

Account Name	Account #	Amount Due	Date Received	Payment Amount	Next Due Date
_____	_____	$ _____	_____	$_____	_____
_____	_____	$ _____	_____	$_____	_____
_____	_____	$ _____	_____	$_____	_____
_____	_____	$ _____	_____	$_____	_____
_____	_____	$ _____	_____	$_____	_____
_____	_____	$ _____	_____	$_____	_____
_____	_____	$ _____	_____	$_____	_____
_____	_____	$ _____	_____	$_____	_____
_____	_____	$ _____	_____	$_____	_____
_____	_____	$ _____	_____	$_____	_____
_____	_____	$ _____	_____	$_____	_____
_____	_____	$ _____	_____	$_____	_____
_____	_____	$ _____	_____	$_____	_____
_____	_____	$ _____	_____	$_____	_____
_____	_____	$ _____	_____	$_____	_____
_____	_____	$ _____	_____	$_____	_____
_____	_____	$ _____	_____	$_____	_____
_____	_____	$ _____	_____	$_____	_____
_____	_____	$ _____	_____	$_____	_____
_____	_____	$ _____	_____	$_____	_____

Total Due: $ _____   **Total Received:** $ _____

ADDITIONAL VALUABLE ASSETS

Name: _____

Valuable Asset: _____

Asset Description: _____

_____

Purchase Date: _____ Purchase Price: $ _____

Present Value: $ _____ Date Sold: _____ Price Sold: $_____

Location of Asset and/or Records: _____

Additional Information: _____

Name: _____

Valuable Asset: _____

Asset Description: _____

_____

Purchase Date: _____ Purchase Price: $ _____

Present Value: $ _____ Date Sold: _____ Price Sold: $_____

Location of Asset and/or Records: _____

Additional Information: _____

Name: _____

Valuable Asset: _____

Asset Description: _____

_____

Purchase Date: _____ Purchase Price: $ _____

Present Value: $ _____ Date Sold: _____ Price Sold: $_____

Location of Asset and/or Records: _____

Additional Information: _____

Form A502

ANNUAL EXPENSE SUMMARY

Name: _____   Year: _____

INCOME	Last Year	This Year	Next Year
Salaries	$ _____	$ _____	$ _____
Commissions/Bonuses	_____	_____	_____
Interest	_____	_____	_____
Alimony	_____	_____	_____
Child Support	_____	_____	_____
Rent	_____	_____	_____
Property Sales	_____	_____	_____
Royalties	_____	_____	_____
Security Sales	_____	_____	_____
Trust Fund	_____	_____	_____
Annuities	_____	_____	_____
Pensions	_____	_____	_____
Social Security	_____	_____	_____
Other: _____	_____	_____	_____
	_____	_____	_____
Total Income	$ _____	$ _____	$ _____
TAXES			
Property Taxes	$ _____	$ _____	$ _____
Social Security	_____	_____	_____
State/City Income Tax	_____	_____	_____
Federal Income Tax	_____	_____	_____
Total Tax Expenditures	$ _____	$ _____	$ _____
LIVING EXPENSES			
Mortgage/Rent	$ _____	$ _____	$ _____
Food	_____	_____	_____
Utilities: Electric	_____	_____	_____
Heat	_____	_____	_____
Water	_____	_____	_____
Phone	_____	_____	_____
Other: _____	_____	_____	_____
	_____	_____	_____
Credit Cards: _____	_____	_____	_____
	_____	_____	_____
	_____	_____	_____
Insurance: Health	_____	_____	_____
Life	_____	_____	_____
Auto	_____	_____	_____
Loans: _____	_____	_____	_____
	_____	_____	_____
Personal/Health Care	_____	_____	_____
Clothing/Maint.	_____	_____	_____
Child Care	_____	_____	_____
Education	_____	_____	_____
Home Maintenance	_____	_____	_____
Membership Fees	_____	_____	_____
Entertainment/Rec.	_____	_____	_____
Contributions	_____	_____	_____
Investments	_____	_____	_____
Savings	_____	_____	_____
Auto: Maintenance	_____	_____	_____
Loan	_____	_____	_____
Gas	_____	_____	_____
Legal Expenses	_____	_____	_____
Other: _____	_____	_____	_____
Total Living Expenses	$ _____	$ _____	$ _____

BANK ACCOUNT RECORD

Name: _____

Name of Bank	Date	Type of Account	Account #	Balance	Interest Rate
_____	_____	_____	_____	$ _____	_____
_____	_____	_____	_____	$ _____	_____
_____	_____	_____	_____	$ _____	_____
_____	_____	_____	_____	$ _____	_____
_____	_____	_____	_____	$ _____	_____
_____	_____	_____	_____	$ _____	_____
_____	_____	_____	_____	$ _____	_____
_____	_____	_____	_____	$ _____	_____
_____	_____	_____	_____	$ _____	_____
_____	_____	_____	_____	$ _____	_____
_____	_____	_____	_____	$ _____	_____
_____	_____	_____	_____	$ _____	_____
_____	_____	_____	_____	$ _____	_____
_____	_____	_____	_____	$ _____	_____
_____	_____	_____	_____	$ _____	_____
_____	_____	_____	_____	$ _____	_____
_____	_____	_____	_____	$ _____	_____
_____	_____	_____	_____	$ _____	_____
_____	_____	_____	_____	$ _____	_____
_____	_____	_____	_____	$ _____	_____
_____	_____	_____	_____	$ _____	_____
_____	_____	_____	_____	$ _____	_____
_____	_____	_____	_____	$ _____	_____

Form B501

BOND PURCHASE LEDGER

Purchaser's Name:_____ Date: _____

Purchase Period:_____ to _____

Type of Bond:_____ Issued by:_____

Date of Purchase: _____ Face Value:_____

Broker:_____ Purchase Price: $ _____ Coupon Rate: _____

Type of Bond:_____ Issued by:_____

Date of Purchase: _____ Face Value:_____

Broker:_____ Purchase Price: $ _____ Coupon Rate: _____

Type of Bond:_____ Issued by:_____

Date of Purchase: _____ Face Value:_____

Broker:_____ Purchase Price: $ _____ Coupon Rate: _____

Type of Bond:_____ Issued by:_____

Date of Purchase: _____ Face Value:_____

Broker:_____ Purchase Price: $ _____ Coupon Rate: _____

Type of Bond:_____ Issued by:_____

Date of Purchase: _____ Face Value:_____

Broker:_____ Purchase Price: $ _____ Coupon Rate: _____

Type of Bond:_____ Issued by:_____

Date of Purchase: _____ Face Value:_____

Broker:_____ Purchase Price: $ _____ Coupon Rate: _____

CERTIFICATES OF DEPOSIT

Name: _____

CD Account #: _____

Purchase Date: _____ Principal: $_____

Interest Rate: _____ Maturity Rate: _____

Banking Institution: _____

Address: _____

Contact: _____ Phone:_____

Certificate/Book Location: _____

Additional Details: _____

_____

_____

_____

Name: _____

CD Account #: _____

Purchase Date: _____ Principal: $_____

Interest Rate: _____ Maturity Rate: _____

Banking Institution: _____

Address: _____

Contact: _____ Phone:_____

Certificate/Book Location: _____

Additional Details: _____

_____

_____

_____

Form C501

CERTIFICATES OF DEPOSIT LIST

Name: _____

Certificate	Date Purchased	Interest Rate	Profit Margin

CHARGE ACCOUNT SUMMARY

Charge/Credit Account: _____ Annual Fee: $_____

Account #: _____ Expiration Date: _____

Authorized Users: _____

Credit Limit: $_____ Interest Rate: _____

Lost Card/Customer Service #: _____

Payment: $ _____ Payment Due: _____ Balance: $ _____

Charge/Credit Account: _____ Annual Fee: $_____

Account #: _____ Expiration Date: _____

Authorized Users: _____

Credit Limit: $_____ Interest Rate: _____

Lost Card/Customer Service #: _____

Payment: $ _____ Payment Due: _____ Balance: $ _____

Charge/Credit Account: _____ Annual Fee: $_____

Account #: _____ Expiration Date: _____

Authorized Users: _____

Credit Limit: $_____ Interest Rate: _____

Lost Card/Customer Service #: _____

Payment: $ _____ Payment Due: _____ Balance: $ _____

Charge/Credit Account: _____ Annual Fee: $_____

Account #: _____ Expiration Date: _____

Authorized Users: _____

Credit Limit: $_____ Interest Rate: _____

Lost Card/Customer Service #: _____

Payment: $ _____ Payment Due: _____ Balance: $ _____

Form C503

CHARITABLE CONTRIBUTIONS

Name: _____ Date: _____

Institution: _____ Donation Period: _____ to _____

Donor	Date	Donation
_____	_____	$ _____
_____	_____	$ _____
_____	_____	$ _____
_____	_____	$ _____
_____	_____	$ _____
_____	_____	$ _____
_____	_____	$ _____
_____	_____	$ _____
_____	_____	$ _____
_____	_____	$ _____
_____	_____	$ _____
_____	_____	$ _____
_____	_____	$ _____
_____	_____	$ _____
_____	_____	$ _____
_____	_____	$ _____
_____	_____	$ _____
_____	_____	$ _____
_____	_____	$ _____
_____	_____	$ _____
_____	_____	$ _____
	Total:	$ _____

CORPORATE/MUNICIPAL BONDS RECORD

Name: _____

Type of Bond	Series #	Date Purchased	Purchase Price	Date of Maturity
_____	_____	_____	$ _____	_____
_____	_____	_____	$ _____	_____
_____	_____	_____	$ _____	_____
_____	_____	_____	$ _____	_____
_____	_____	_____	$ _____	_____
_____	_____	_____	$ _____	_____
_____	_____	_____	$ _____	_____
_____	_____	_____	$ _____	_____
_____	_____	_____	$ _____	_____
_____	_____	_____	$ _____	_____
_____	_____	_____	$ _____	_____
_____	_____	_____	$ _____	_____
_____	_____	_____	$ _____	_____
_____	_____	_____	$ _____	_____
_____	_____	_____	$ _____	_____
_____	_____	_____	$ _____	_____
_____	_____	_____	$ _____	_____
_____	_____	_____	$ _____	_____
_____	_____	_____	$ _____	_____
_____	_____	_____	$ _____	_____
_____	_____	_____	$ _____	_____
_____	_____	_____	$ _____	_____

Form C505

DEPOSIT BOX CONTENTS LOG

Name: _____

Safety Deposit Box Location: _____

Address: _____

_____

Box #: _____ Location of Key: _____

Owners/Keyholders: _____

_____

Date	Inventory of Box Contents	Value
_____	_____	$_____
_____	_____	$_____
_____	_____	$_____
_____	_____	$_____
_____	_____	$_____
_____	_____	$_____
_____	_____	$_____
_____	_____	$_____
_____	_____	$_____
_____	_____	$_____
_____	_____	$_____
_____	_____	$_____
_____	_____	$_____
_____	_____	$_____
_____	_____	$_____
_____	_____	$_____
_____	_____	$_____
_____	_____	$_____
		Total: $_____

DISABILITY INSURANCE RECORD

Name of Insured: _____

Policy #1

Company: _____

Policy #: _____ Type: _____

Benefits: _____

_____

Expires: _____ Annual Premium: $ _____ Due: _____

Policy #2

Company: _____

Policy #: _____ Type: _____

Benefits: _____

_____

Expires: _____ Annual Premium: $ _____ Due: _____

Policy #3

Company: _____

Policy #: _____ Type: _____

Benefits: _____

_____

Expires: _____ Annual Premium: $ _____ Due: _____

Policy #4

Company: _____

Policy #: _____ Type: _____

Benefits: _____

_____

Expires: _____ Annual Premium: $ _____ Due: _____

Form D502

EXPENSE REIMBURSEMENT FORM

Name: _____

Item	Cost	Purchase Date	Reimbursement Date
_____	$ _____	_____	_____
_____	$ _____	_____	_____
_____	$ _____	_____	_____
_____	$ _____	_____	_____
_____	$ _____	_____	_____
_____	$ _____	_____	_____
_____	$ _____	_____	_____
_____	$ _____	_____	_____
_____	$ _____	_____	_____
_____	$ _____	_____	_____
_____	$ _____	_____	_____
_____	$ _____	_____	_____
_____	$ _____	_____	_____
_____	$ _____	_____	_____
_____	$ _____	_____	_____
_____	$ _____	_____	_____
_____	$ _____	_____	_____
_____	$ _____	_____	_____
_____	$ _____	_____	_____
_____	$ _____	_____	_____

Total: $ _____

HISTORY OF LOAN PAYMENTS

Loan Payer: _____ Loan Recipient: _____

Terms: _____

Date Due	Date Paid	Amount	Balance
_____	_____	$_____	$_____
_____	_____	$_____	$_____
_____	_____	$_____	$_____
_____	_____	$_____	$_____
_____	_____	$_____	$_____
_____	_____	$_____	$_____
_____	_____	$_____	$_____
_____	_____	$_____	$_____
_____	_____	$_____	$_____
_____	_____	$_____	$_____
_____	_____	$_____	$_____
_____	_____	$_____	$_____
_____	_____	$_____	$_____
_____	_____	$_____	$_____
_____	_____	$_____	$_____
_____	_____	$_____	$_____
_____	_____	$_____	$_____
_____	_____	$_____	$_____
_____	_____	$_____	$_____
_____	_____	$_____	$_____
_____	_____	$_____	$_____
		$_____	$_____

Form H501

INSURED PROPERTY LIST

Name: _____

Insured Property Description	Policy/ Rider	Insured Value
_____	_____	$_____
_____	_____	$_____
_____	_____	$_____
_____	_____	$_____
_____	_____	$_____
_____	_____	$_____
_____	_____	$_____
_____	_____	$_____
_____	_____	$_____
_____	_____	$_____
_____	_____	$_____
_____	_____	$_____
_____	_____	$_____
_____	_____	$_____
_____	_____	$_____
_____	_____	$_____
_____	_____	$_____
_____	_____	$_____
_____	_____	$_____
_____	_____	$_____
_____	_____	$_____
_____	_____	$_____
_____	_____	$_____

INTEREST PAYMENTS

Name: _____

For the Month Of: _____ Year: _____

Paid to	Date	Total	Principal	Interest
_____	_____	$ _____	$ _____	$ _____
_____	_____	$ _____	$ _____	$ _____
_____	_____	$ _____	$ _____	$ _____
_____	_____	$ _____	$ _____	$ _____
_____	_____	$ _____	$ _____	$ _____
_____	_____	$ _____	$ _____	$ _____
_____	_____	$ _____	$ _____	$ _____
_____	_____	$ _____	$ _____	$ _____
_____	_____	$ _____	$ _____	$ _____
_____	_____	$ _____	$ _____	$ _____
_____	_____	$ _____	$ _____	$ _____
_____	_____	$ _____	$ _____	$ _____
_____	_____	$ _____	$ _____	$ _____
_____	_____	$ _____	$ _____	$ _____
_____	_____	$ _____	$ _____	$ _____
_____	_____	$ _____	$ _____	$ _____
_____	_____	$ _____	$ _____	$ _____
_____	_____	$ _____	$ _____	$ _____
_____	_____	$ _____	$ _____	$ _____
_____	_____	$ _____	$ _____	$ _____
_____	_____	$ _____	$ _____	$ _____
Monthly Totals:		$ _____	$ _____	$ _____

Form I502

INVESTMENT GAINS AND LOSSES

Name: _____

Time Period Covered: _____ to_____

Investment Description	Price Paid	Price Sold	Gain or Loss	Date Purchased	Date Sold
_____	$ _____	$_____	$_____	_____	_____
_____	$ _____	$_____	$_____	_____	_____
_____	$ _____	$_____	$_____	_____	_____
_____	$ _____	$_____	$_____	_____	_____
_____	$ _____	$_____	$_____	_____	_____
_____	$ _____	$_____	$_____	_____	_____
_____	$ _____	$_____	$_____	_____	_____
_____	$ _____	$_____	$_____	_____	_____
_____	$ _____	$_____	$_____	_____	_____
_____	$ _____	$_____	$_____	_____	_____
_____	$ _____	$_____	$_____	_____	_____
_____	$ _____	$_____	$_____	_____	_____
_____	$ _____	$_____	$_____	_____	_____
_____	$ _____	$_____	$_____	_____	_____
_____	$ _____	$_____	$_____	_____	_____
_____	$ _____	$_____	$_____	_____	_____
_____	$ _____	$_____	$_____	_____	_____
_____	$ _____	$_____	$_____	_____	_____
_____	$ _____	$_____	$_____	_____	_____
_____	$ _____	$_____	$_____	_____	_____
_____	$ _____	$_____	$_____	_____	_____

INVESTMENT SECURITIES

Name: _____

Security Description	# Shares	Purchase Date	Maturity Date	Purchase Price	Current Value
_____	_____	_____	_____	$_____	$_____
_____	_____	_____	_____	$_____	$_____
_____	_____	_____	_____	$_____	$_____
_____	_____	_____	_____	$_____	$_____
_____	_____	_____	_____	$_____	$_____
_____	_____	_____	_____	$_____	$_____
_____	_____	_____	_____	$_____	$_____
_____	_____	_____	_____	$_____	$_____
_____	_____	_____	_____	$_____	$_____
_____	_____	_____	_____	$_____	$_____
_____	_____	_____	_____	$_____	$_____
_____	_____	_____	_____	$_____	$_____
_____	_____	_____	_____	$_____	$_____
_____	_____	_____	_____	$_____	$_____
_____	_____	_____	_____	$_____	$_____
_____	_____	_____	_____	$_____	$_____
_____	_____	_____	_____	$_____	$_____
_____	_____	_____	_____	$_____	$_____
_____	_____	_____	_____	$_____	$_____
_____	_____	_____	_____	$_____	$_____
_____	_____	_____	_____	$_____	$_____
_____	_____	_____	_____	$_____	$_____

Form I504

KEOGHS AND IRAS

Name: _____

Plan Description: _____ Account #: _____

Date Account Opened: _____ Current Balance: $_____

Where Invested: _____

Account Supervisor: _____ Phone: _____

Address: _____

_____

Trustee/Beneficiary: _____

Document Location: _____

Additional Information: _____

_____

_____

Name: _____

Plan Description: _____ Account #: _____

Date Account Opened: _____ Current Balance: $_____

Where Invested: _____

Account Supervisor: _____ Phone: _____

Address: _____

_____

Trustee/Beneficiary: _____

Document Location: _____

Additional Information: _____

_____

_____

LOAN IDENTIFICATION FORM

Name: _____

Loan Type: _____

    Account #: _____ Principal: $ _____

    Interest Rate: _____ Date Borrowed: _____ Term of Loan: _____

    Monthly Payment: $ _____ Date Due: _____

    Date Payments Begin: _____

    Lender: _____

    Address: _____

    Contact: _____ Phone: _____

    Additional Information: _____

    _____

    _____

Loan Type: _____

    Account #: _____ Principal: $ _____

    Interest Rate: _____ Date Borrowed: _____ Term of Loan: _____

    Monthly Payment: $ _____ Date Due: _____

    Date Payments Begin: _____

    Lender: _____

    Address: _____

    Contact: _____ Phone: _____

    Additional Information: _____

    _____

    _____

MONEY MARKET ACCOUNTS

Name: _____

Name of Fund: _____ Account #: _____

Name of Firm: _____

Contact Name: _____ Phone: _____

Date Account Established: _____ Initial Investment: _____

Date of Contribution	Amount of Contribution	Balance
_____	$_____	$_____
_____	$_____	$_____
_____	$_____	$_____
_____	$_____	$_____
_____	$_____	$_____
_____	$_____	$_____
_____	$_____	$_____
_____	$_____	$_____
_____	$_____	$_____
_____	$_____	$_____
_____	$_____	$_____
_____	$_____	$_____
_____	$_____	$_____
_____	$_____	$_____
_____	$_____	$_____
_____	$_____	$_____
_____	$_____	$_____
_____	$_____	$_____
_____	$_____	$_____

MONTHLY EXPENSE SUMMARY

Name:_____ Month: _____ Year: _____

Income

Salaries	$_____
Commissions/ Bonuses	_____
Interest	_____
Dividends	_____
Alimony	_____
Child Support	_____
Rents	_____
Property Sales	_____
Royalties	_____
Security	_____
Sales	_____
Trust Funds	_____
Annuities	_____
Pensions	_____
Social Security	_____
Other: _____	_____
_____	_____
_____	_____
_____	_____
_____	_____
Total Income	$_____

Expenses

Mortgage/Rent	$_____
Utilities: Heat	_____
Elec.	_____
Water	_____
Phone	_____
Other:_____	_____
Home Maintenance	_____
Food	_____
Auto: Loan	_____
Maint.	_____
Gas	_____
Insurance	_____
Credit Cards:	_____
_____	_____
_____	_____
Insurance: Life	_____
Auto	_____
Health	_____
Loans:	_____
	_____
Clothing/Toiletries	_____
Medical	_____
Dental/Optical	_____
Child Care	_____
Education	_____
Membership Fees	_____
Entertainment/Rec.	_____
Contributions	_____
Property Tax	_____
Income Tax	_____
Investments/Savings	_____
Legal Expenses	_____
Other:_____	_____
_____	_____
Total Expenses	$_____

Form M502

MONTHLY PAYMENT SCHEDULE

For The Month Of: _____

Company	Total Balance	Payment Due	Due Date	Paid Date	Method of Payment	Pd. ☐
Credit Cards						
_____	_____	_____	_____	_____	_____	☐
_____	_____	_____	_____	_____	_____	☐
_____	_____	_____	_____	_____	_____	☐
_____	_____	_____	_____	_____	_____	☐
_____	_____	_____	_____	_____	_____	☐
_____	_____	_____	_____	_____	_____	☐
_____	_____	_____	_____	_____	_____	☐
_____	_____	_____	_____	_____	_____	☐
_____	_____	_____	_____	_____	_____	☐
Utilities						
_____	_____	_____	_____	_____	_____	☐
_____	_____	_____	_____	_____	_____	☐
_____	_____	_____	_____	_____	_____	☐
_____	_____	_____	_____	_____	_____	☐
Store/Gas Cards						
_____	_____	_____	_____	_____	_____	☐
_____	_____	_____	_____	_____	_____	☐
_____	_____	_____	_____	_____	_____	☐
_____	_____	_____	_____	_____	_____	☐
Mortgage/Car Payments						
_____	_____	_____	_____	_____	_____	☐
_____	_____	_____	_____	_____	_____	☐

OUTSTANDING DEBTS

Borrower's Name: _____ Date: _____

Lender	Phone	Reason for Loan	Debt	Date Due
_____	_____	_____	$_____	_____
_____	_____	_____	$_____	_____
_____	_____	_____	$_____	_____
_____	_____	_____	$_____	_____
_____	_____	_____	$_____	_____
_____	_____	_____	$_____	_____
_____	_____	_____	$_____	_____
_____	_____	_____	$_____	_____
_____	_____	_____	$_____	_____
_____	_____	_____	$_____	_____
_____	_____	_____	$_____	_____
_____	_____	_____	$_____	_____
_____	_____	_____	$_____	_____
_____	_____	_____	$_____	_____
_____	_____	_____	$_____	_____
_____	_____	_____	$_____	_____
_____	_____	_____	$_____	_____
_____	_____	_____	$_____	_____
_____	_____	_____	$_____	_____
_____	_____	_____	$_____	_____

Total: $_____

Form O501

PENSION CONTRIBUTION LOG

Contributor Name: _____

Investment Type: _____

Year: _____

Month	Contribution	Earnings	Withdrawals
January:	$_____	$_____	$_____
February:	_____	_____	_____
March:	_____	_____	_____
April:	_____	_____	_____
May:	_____	_____	_____
June:	_____	_____	_____
July:	_____	_____	_____
August:	_____	_____	_____
September:	_____	_____	_____
October:	_____	_____	_____
November:	_____	_____	_____
December:	_____	_____	_____
Total:	$_____	$_____	$_____

PERSONAL FINANCIAL STATEMENT

Name:_____ Date: _____

Assets:

Cash $_____

Checking Account(s) $_____

Savings Account(s) $_____

Other Savings (CDs, etc.) $_____

House (market value) $_____

Other Real Estate (market value) $_____

Household Furnishings (market value) $_____

Automobile(s) (blue book value) $_____

Life Insurance (cash value) $_____

Stocks, Bonds (current value) $_____

Retirement Plans/Profit Sharing $_____

Other Assets $_____

Total Assets: $_____

Debts:

Mortgages (balance due) $_____

Installment Loans (balance due) $_____

Other Loans (balance due) $_____

Credit Cards (balance due) $_____

Charge Accounts (amount owed) $_____

Insurance Premiums Due $_____

Taxes Owed to Date $_____

Total Debts: $_____

Net Worth (Total Assets minus Total Debts): $_____

 Form P502

PHILANTHROPIC DONATIONS

Contributor: _____

Donation Period: _____ to _____

Recipient	Date	Contribution	Dollar Amount	Value of Goods
_____	_____	_____	$ _____	$ _____
_____	_____	_____	$ _____	$ _____
_____	_____	_____	$ _____	$ _____
_____	_____	_____	$ _____	$ _____
_____	_____	_____	$ _____	$ _____
_____	_____	_____	$ _____	$ _____
_____	_____	_____	$ _____	$ _____
_____	_____	_____	$ _____	$ _____
_____	_____	_____	$ _____	$ _____
_____	_____	_____	$ _____	$ _____
_____	_____	_____	$ _____	$ _____
_____	_____	_____	$ _____	$ _____
_____	_____	_____	$ _____	$ _____
_____	_____	_____	$ _____	$ _____
_____	_____	_____	$ _____	$ _____
_____	_____	_____	$ _____	$ _____
_____	_____	_____	$ _____	$ _____
_____	_____	_____	$ _____	$ _____
_____	_____	_____	$ _____	$ _____
_____	_____	_____	$ _____	$ _____
_____	_____	_____	$ _____	$ _____
_____	_____	_____	$ _____	$ _____

Total: $ _____ $ _____

PRECIOUS METALS, GEMSTONES, AND JEWELRY RECORD

Name: _____

Purchase Date	Type of Metal, Jewelry or Gem	Purchased From	Purchase Price	Current Location
_____	_____	_____	$_____	_____
_____	_____	_____	$_____	_____
_____	_____	_____	$_____	_____
_____	_____	_____	$_____	_____
_____	_____	_____	$_____	_____
_____	_____	_____	$_____	_____
_____	_____	_____	$_____	_____
_____	_____	_____	$_____	_____
_____	_____	_____	$_____	_____
_____	_____	_____	$_____	_____
_____	_____	_____	$_____	_____
_____	_____	_____	$_____	_____
_____	_____	_____	$_____	_____
_____	_____	_____	$_____	_____
_____	_____	_____	$_____	_____
_____	_____	_____	$_____	_____
_____	_____	_____	$_____	_____
_____	_____	_____	$_____	_____
_____	_____	_____	$_____	_____
_____	_____	_____	$_____	_____
_____	_____	_____	$_____	_____

Form P506

PROPERTY AND LIABILITY INSURANCE COVERAGE

Name of Insured: _____

Property Covered: _____

Property Description: _____

_____

Address: _____

_____

Insurance Provider: _____ Policy #: _____

Coverage

Dwelling Amount: $ _____ Other Buildings: $ _____

Personal Property: $ _____ Living Expense: $_____

Personal Liability: $ _____ Public Liability: $_____

Deductibles: $ _____ Premium: $ _____

Premium Due: _____ Expires: _____

Additional Coverages: _____

_____

_____

Insurance Agent: _____ Phone: _____

Address: _____

Policyholder Service or Claims Phone: _____

Insurance Policy Location: _____

Property Inventory Location: _____

Additional Information: _____

_____

_____

_____

RECORD OF INCOME

Name: _____

Quarter: _____ Year: _____

Week Ending	Hours		Deductions			Net Pay
	Reg.	O.T.	Fed. W.H.	St. W.H.	FICA	
_____	_____	_____	$ _____	$ _____	$ _____	$ _____
_____	_____	_____	$ _____	$ _____	$ _____	$ _____
_____	_____	_____	$ _____	$ _____	$ _____	$ _____
_____	_____	_____	$ _____	$ _____	$ _____	$ _____
_____	_____	_____	$ _____	$ _____	$ _____	$ _____
_____	_____	_____	$ _____	$ _____	$ _____	$ _____
_____	_____	_____	$ _____	$ _____	$ _____	$ _____
_____	_____	_____	$ _____	$ _____	$ _____	$ _____
_____	_____	_____	$ _____	$ _____	$ _____	$ _____
_____	_____	_____	$ _____	$ _____	$ _____	$ _____
_____	_____	_____	$ _____	$ _____	$ _____	$ _____
_____	_____	_____	$ _____	$ _____	$ _____	$ _____
_____	_____	_____	$ _____	$ _____	$ _____	$ _____
_____	_____	_____	$ _____	$ _____	$ _____	$ _____
_____	_____	_____	$ _____	$ _____	$ _____	$ _____
_____	_____	_____	$ _____	$ _____	$ _____	$ _____
_____	_____	_____	$ _____	$ _____	$ _____	$ _____
Quarter Total:	_____	_____	$ _____	$ _____	$ _____	$ _____

Form R501

RETIREMENT EXPENSES

Name:_____ Year:_____

	Yourself	Spouse	Total
Living Expenses			
Rent/Mortgage Payment	$ _____	$ _____	$ _____
Food	_____	_____	_____
Clothing	_____	_____	_____
Utilities	_____	_____	_____
Home Maint./Improvements	_____	_____	_____
Auto/Transportation	_____	_____	_____
Membership Fees	_____	_____	_____
Entertainment/Rec.	_____	_____	_____
Furniture/Durable Goods	_____	_____	_____
Medical Expenses	_____	_____	_____
Charge Card Payments	_____	_____	_____
Travel	_____	_____	_____
Insurance: Auto	_____	_____	_____
Life	_____	_____	_____
Health	_____	_____	_____
Legal Fees	_____	_____	_____
Loan Payments	_____	_____	_____
Other:_____	_____	_____	_____
Total Living Expenses	$ _____	$ _____	$ _____
Income			
Social Security	$ _____	$ _____	$ _____
Pension Plan	_____	_____	_____
Profit Sharing	_____	_____	_____
IRA/Keogh	_____	_____	_____
Private Annuity	_____	_____	_____
Interest on Savings	_____	_____	_____
Interest on Bonds	_____	_____	_____
Stock Dividends	_____	_____	_____
Rental Income	_____	_____	_____
Other:_____	_____	_____	_____
Total Income	$ _____	$ _____	$ _____
Taxes			
Federal Income Tax	$ _____	$ _____	$ _____
State/City Income Tax	_____	_____	_____
Property Taxes	_____	_____	_____
Total Taxes	$ _____	$ _____	$ _____

RETURNS ON INVESTMENTS

Name: _____

Time Period Covered: _____

Date Return Received	Total Amount Invested	Investment Source	Return on Investment
_____	$_____	_____	$_____
_____	$_____	_____	$_____
_____	$_____	_____	$_____
_____	$_____	_____	$_____
_____	$_____	_____	$_____
_____	$_____	_____	$_____
_____	$_____	_____	$_____
_____	$_____	_____	$_____
_____	$_____	_____	$_____
_____	$_____	_____	$_____
_____	$_____	_____	$_____
_____	$_____	_____	$_____
_____	$_____	_____	$_____
_____	$_____	_____	$_____
_____	$_____	_____	$_____
_____	$_____	_____	$_____
_____	$_____	_____	$_____
_____	$_____	_____	$_____
_____	$_____	_____	$_____
_____	$_____	_____	$_____

Form R503

SALE OF BONDS

Seller's Name: _____

Date of Sale: _____ Purchaser: _____

Bond:_____ Type of Bond: _____

Coupon Rate: _____

Face Value: $ _____ Selling Price: $ _____

Date of Sale: _____ Purchaser: _____

Bond:_____ Type of Bond: _____

Coupon Rate: _____

Face Value: $ _____ Selling Price: $ _____

Date of Sale: _____ Purchaser: _____

Bond:_____ Type of Bond: _____

Coupon Rate: _____

Face Value: $ _____ Selling Price: $ _____

Date of Sale: _____ Purchaser: _____

Bond:_____ Type of Bond: _____

Coupon Rate: _____

Face Value: $ _____ Selling Price: $ _____

Date of Sale: _____ Purchaser: _____

Bond:_____ Type of Bond: _____

Coupon Rate: _____

Face Value: $ _____ Selling Price: $ _____

SAVINGS BONDS COLLECTION

Name: _____

Description	Bond #	Issue Date	Issue Price	Exp. Date
_____	_____	_____	$ _____	_____
_____	_____	_____	$ _____	_____
_____	_____	_____	$ _____	_____
_____	_____	_____	$ _____	_____
_____	_____	_____	$ _____	_____
_____	_____	_____	$ _____	_____
_____	_____	_____	$ _____	_____
_____	_____	_____	$ _____	_____
_____	_____	_____	$ _____	_____
_____	_____	_____	$ _____	_____
_____	_____	_____	$ _____	_____
_____	_____	_____	$ _____	_____
_____	_____	_____	$ _____	_____
_____	_____	_____	$ _____	_____
_____	_____	_____	$ _____	_____
_____	_____	_____	$ _____	_____
_____	_____	_____	$ _____	_____
_____	_____	_____	$ _____	_____
_____	_____	_____	$ _____	_____
_____	_____	_____	$ _____	_____
_____	_____	_____	$ _____	_____
_____	_____	_____	$ _____	_____

170   **Form S502**

SAVINGS/CHECKING ACCOUNT RECORD

Account Holder: _____ Date: _____

Savings Account #: _____ Date Opened: _____

Bank: _____ Branch: _____

Branch Address: _____

_____ Phone: _____

Savings Account Balance: $ _____

Minimum Amount Allowed: $ _____

Applicable Charges: $ _____

Interest Rate: _____

Authorized Signatures: _____

Additional Terms: _____

Account Holder: _____ Date: _____

Checking Account #: _____ Date Opened: _____

Bank: _____ Branch: _____

Branch Address: _____

_____ Phone: _____

Checking Account Balance: $ _____

Monthly Charges: $ _____ with Minimum Amount of: $ _____

Per Check Charges: $_____ ATM Charge: $ _____ Overdraft Charge: $ _____

Interest Rate: _____

Authorized Signatures: _____

Additional Terms: _____

SCHEDULE OF BENEFICIARIES
AND DISTRIBUTIVE SHARES

The following are the named beneficiaries of the _____

Trust, as of this _____ day of _____ , _____ (year).

Name of Beneficiary

Property to be Distributed and
Quantity and/or Percent

_____   _____

_____   _____

_____   _____

_____   _____

_____   _____

_____   _____

_____   _____

_____   _____

_____   _____

_____   _____

_____   _____

_____   _____

_____   _____

Form S508

SCHEDULE OF TRUST ASSETS

Name of Trust: _____   Date of Trust: _____

No.	Date of transfer	Asset transferred into trust	Form of ownership	Tax based on date of transfer	Fair Market Value on date of transfer
____	_____	_____	_____	_____	_____
____	_____	_____	_____	_____	_____
____	_____	_____	_____	_____	_____
____	_____	_____	_____	_____	_____
____	_____	_____	_____	_____	_____
____	_____	_____	_____	_____	_____
____	_____	_____	_____	_____	_____
____	_____	_____	_____	_____	_____
____	_____	_____	_____	_____	_____
____	_____	_____	_____	_____	_____
____	_____	_____	_____	_____	_____
____	_____	_____	_____	_____	_____
____	_____	_____	_____	_____	_____
____	_____	_____	_____	_____	_____
____	_____	_____	_____	_____	_____
____	_____	_____	_____	_____	_____
____	_____	_____	_____	_____	_____
____	_____	_____	_____	_____	_____
____	_____	_____	_____	_____	_____
____	_____	_____	_____	_____	_____

The undersigned Grantor(s) has(ve) reviewed the Schedule of Assets and approve the form of ownership of property as set forth above this date:_____

_____   _____
Signature of Grantor   Signature of Grantor

SOCIAL SECURITY REGISTRY

Name:_____ Social Security #:_____

Date Benefits Begin:_____

Date	Amount Contributed	Comments
_____	$ _____	_____
_____	$ _____	_____
_____	$ _____	_____
_____	$ _____	_____
_____	$ _____	_____
_____	$ _____	_____
_____	$ _____	_____
_____	$ _____	_____
_____	$ _____	_____
_____	$ _____	_____
_____	$ _____	_____
_____	$ _____	_____
_____	$ _____	_____
_____	$ _____	_____
_____	$ _____	_____
_____	$ _____	_____
_____	$ _____	_____
_____	$ _____	_____
_____	$ _____	_____
_____	$ _____	_____
_____	$ _____	_____

Form S504

STOCK PURCHASES

Name of Purchaser:_____

Date Bought	Stock	# of Shares	Price/ Share	Price Paid	Broker
_____	_____	_____	$_____	$_____	_____
_____	_____	_____	$_____	$_____	_____
_____	_____	_____	$_____	$_____	_____
_____	_____	_____	$_____	$_____	_____
_____	_____	_____	$_____	$_____	_____
_____	_____	_____	$_____	$_____	_____
_____	_____	_____	$_____	$_____	_____
_____	_____	_____	$_____	$_____	_____
_____	_____	_____	$_____	$_____	_____
_____	_____	_____	$_____	$_____	_____
_____	_____	_____	$_____	$_____	_____
_____	_____	_____	$_____	$_____	_____
_____	_____	_____	$_____	$_____	_____
_____	_____	_____	$_____	$_____	_____
_____	_____	_____	$_____	$_____	_____
_____	_____	_____	$_____	$_____	_____
_____	_____	_____	$_____	$_____	_____
_____	_____	_____	$_____	$_____	_____
_____	_____	_____	$_____	$_____	_____
_____	_____	_____	$_____	$_____	_____
_____	_____	_____	$_____	$_____	_____

Total: $_____

STOCK SALES

Name of Seller: _____

Date Sold	Stock	# of Shares	Price/ Share	Price Sold	Broker
_____	_____	_____	$ _____	$ _____	_____
_____	_____	_____	$ _____	$ _____	_____
_____	_____	_____	$ _____	$ _____	_____
_____	_____	_____	$ _____	$ _____	_____
_____	_____	_____	$ _____	$ _____	_____
_____	_____	_____	$ _____	$ _____	_____
_____	_____	_____	$ _____	$ _____	_____
_____	_____	_____	$ _____	$ _____	_____
_____	_____	_____	$ _____	$ _____	_____
_____	_____	_____	$ _____	$ _____	_____
_____	_____	_____	$ _____	$ _____	_____
_____	_____	_____	$ _____	$ _____	_____
_____	_____	_____	$ _____	$ _____	_____
_____	_____	_____	$ _____	$ _____	_____
_____	_____	_____	$ _____	$ _____	_____
_____	_____	_____	$ _____	$ _____	_____
_____	_____	_____	$ _____	$ _____	_____
_____	_____	_____	$ _____	$ _____	_____
_____	_____	_____	$ _____	$ _____	_____
_____	_____	_____	$ _____	$ _____	_____
_____	_____	_____	$ _____	$ _____	_____
_____	_____	_____	$ _____	$ _____	
_____	_____	_____	$ _____	$ _____	

Total: $ _____

Form S507

TALLY OF DAY-BY-DAY CLOSING BALANCES

Name: _____

	Security	Security	Security	Security
	_____	_____	_____	_____
Day: _____	C_____	C_____	C_____	C_____
	A_____	A_____	A_____	A_____
Day: _____	C_____	C_____	C_____	C_____
	A_____	A_____	A_____	A_____
Day: _____	C_____	C_____	C_____	C_____
	A_____	A_____	A_____	A_____
Day: _____	C_____	C_____	C_____	C_____
	A_____	A_____	A_____	A_____
Day: _____	C_____	C_____	C_____	C_____
	A_____	A_____	A_____	A_____
Day: _____	C_____	C_____	C_____	C_____
	A_____	A_____	A_____	A_____
Day: _____	C_____	C_____	C_____	C_____
	A_____	A_____	A_____	A_____
Day: _____	C_____	C_____	C_____	C_____
	A_____	A_____	A_____	A_____
Day: _____	C_____	C_____	C_____	C_____
	A_____	A_____	A_____	A_____
Day: _____	C_____	C_____	C_____	C_____
	A_____	A_____	A_____	A_____

C = Closing Price   A = Accounts Value

TAX RECORD FINDER

Name: _____

Current Year: _____

Tax Preparation Service Used: _____

Address: _____

Contact: _____ Phone: _____

Amount Expected to Owe/Receive: $_____

Location of Income Documentation: _____

_____

Location of Expense Documentation: _____

_____

Additional Information: _____

_____

Previous Year: _____

Tax Preparation Service Used: _____

Address: _____

Contact: _____ Phone: _____

Amount Owed/Received: $ _____

Location of Income Documentation: _____

_____

Location of Expense Documentation: _____

_____

Additional Information: _____

_____

UNIT INVESTMENT TRUSTS

Name: _____

Name of Trust	Date Purchased	Units Purchased	Purchase Price	Interest Rate	Date Sold	Sale Price
_____	_____	_____	$_____	_____	_____	$_____
_____	_____	_____	$_____	_____	_____	$_____
_____	_____	_____	$_____	_____	_____	$_____
_____	_____	_____	$_____	_____	_____	$_____
_____	_____	_____	$_____	_____	_____	$_____
_____	_____	_____	$_____	_____	_____	$_____
_____	_____	_____	$_____	_____	_____	$_____
_____	_____	_____	$_____	_____	_____	$_____
_____	_____	_____	$_____	_____	_____	$_____
_____	_____	_____	$_____	_____	_____	$_____
_____	_____	_____	$_____	_____	_____	$_____
_____	_____	_____	$_____	_____	_____	$_____
_____	_____	_____	$_____	_____	_____	$_____
_____	_____	_____	$_____	_____	_____	$_____
_____	_____	_____	$_____	_____	_____	$_____
_____	_____	_____	$_____	_____	_____	$_____
_____	_____	_____	$_____	_____	_____	$_____
_____	_____	_____	$_____	_____	_____	$_____
_____	_____	_____	$_____	_____	_____	$_____
_____	_____	_____	$_____	_____	_____	$_____
_____	_____	_____	$_____	_____	_____	$_____
_____	_____	_____	$_____	_____	_____	$_____
_____	_____	_____	$_____	_____	_____	$_____

U.S. SAVINGS/TREASURY BONDS REGISTRY

Name: _____

Type of Bond	Series #	Amount	Purchase Date	Maturity Date
_____	_____	$_____	_____	_____
_____	_____	$_____	_____	_____
_____	_____	$_____	_____	_____
_____	_____	$_____	_____	_____
_____	_____	$_____	_____	_____
_____	_____	$_____	_____	_____
_____	_____	$_____	_____	_____
_____	_____	$_____	_____	_____
_____	_____	$_____	_____	_____
_____	_____	$_____	_____	_____
_____	_____	$_____	_____	_____
_____	_____	$_____	_____	_____
_____	_____	$_____	_____	_____
_____	_____	$_____	_____	_____
_____	_____	$_____	_____	_____
_____	_____	$_____	_____	_____
_____	_____	$_____	_____	_____
_____	_____	$_____	_____	_____
_____	_____	$_____	_____	_____
_____	_____	$_____	_____	_____
_____	_____	$_____	_____	_____
_____	_____	$_____	_____	_____
_____	_____	$_____	_____	_____
_____	_____	$_____	_____	_____

Form U502

WILLS AND TRUSTS

Wills

Name:_____ Date Signed:_____

Attorney: _____ Phone: _____

Attorney Address:_____

_____

Executor of Estate: _____ Phone: _____

Executor Address: _____

_____

Location of Original Will: _____

Location of Copies: _____

Codicils (if any): _____

Additional Information:_____

_____

Trusts

Name:_____ Date of Trust:_____

Trustee(s): _____ Phone:_____

Address: _____

_____

Location of Trust Documents:_____

_____

Location of Copies:_____

Amendments (if any): _____

_____

Additional Information:_____

_____

ZERO COUPON BONDS REGISTRY

Name: _____

Type of Bond	Date Purchased	Purchase Price	Interest Rate	Date of Maturity
_____	_____	$_____	_____	_____
_____	_____	$_____	_____	_____
_____	_____	$_____	_____	_____
_____	_____	$_____	_____	_____
_____	_____	$_____	_____	_____
_____	_____	$_____	_____	_____
_____	_____	$_____	_____	_____
_____	_____	$_____	_____	_____
_____	_____	$_____	_____	_____
_____	_____	$_____	_____	_____
_____	_____	$_____	_____	_____
_____	_____	$_____	_____	_____
_____	_____	$_____	_____	_____
_____	_____	$_____	_____	_____
_____	_____	$_____	_____	_____
_____	_____	$_____	_____	_____
_____	_____	$_____	_____	_____
_____	_____	$_____	_____	_____
_____	_____	$_____	_____	_____
_____	_____	$_____	_____	_____
_____	_____	$_____	_____	_____
_____	_____	$_____	_____	_____
_____	_____	$_____	_____	_____
_____	_____	$_____	_____	_____

Form Z501

Purchase and maintenance records

6

Section 6

Purchase and maintenance records

Forms in this section

CATALOG/MAIL ORDER REGISTER

Name: _____

Item Ordered: _____ Number:_____

Quantity: _____ Price Each: $ _____ Total: $ _____

Ordered From: _____ Phone: _____

Address: _____

Date Ordered: _____ Date Received: _____ Payment Method:_____

Item Ordered: _____ Number:_____

Quantity: _____ Price Each: $ _____ Total: $ _____

Ordered From: _____ Phone: _____

Address: _____

Date Ordered: _____ Date Received: _____ Payment Method:_____

Item Ordered: _____ Number:_____

Quantity: _____ Price Each: $ _____ Total: $ _____

Ordered From: _____ Phone: _____

Address: _____

Date Ordered: _____ Date Received: _____ Payment Method:_____

Item Ordered: _____ Number:_____

Quantity: _____ Price Each: $ _____ Total: $ _____

Ordered From: _____ Phone: _____

Address: _____

Date Ordered: _____ Date Received: _____ Payment Method:_____

EQUIPMENT SERVICE LOG

Equipment/Machinery: _____

Name of Manufacturer: _____

Model: _____ Purchase Date: _____

Serial #: _____ Year: _____ Price: $_____

Purchased From: _____

Address: _____

Phone: _____ Warranty Expires: _____

Service Contract With: _____

Address: _____

Service Record:

Date   Service

_____   _____

_____   _____

_____   _____

_____   _____

_____   _____

_____   _____

_____   _____

_____   _____

_____   _____

_____   _____

_____   _____

_____   _____

GIFT REGISTRY

HOUSEWARES

Item_____ Company _____
Color/Pattern_____

Item_____ Company _____
Color/Pattern_____

Item_____ Company _____
Color/Pattern_____

Item_____ Company _____
Color/Pattern_____

Item_____ Company _____
Color/Pattern_____

Item_____ Company _____
Color/Pattern_____

Item_____ Company _____
Color/Pattern_____

Item_____ Company _____
Color/Pattern_____

BED & BATH

Item_____ Company _____
Color/Pattern_____

Item_____ Company _____
Color/Pattern_____

Item_____ Company _____
Color/Pattern_____

Item_____ Company _____
Color/Pattern_____

Item_____ Company _____
Color/Pattern_____

CHINA & CRYSTAL

Item_____ Company _____
Color/Pattern_____

Item_____ Company _____
Color/Pattern_____

Item_____ Company _____
Color/Pattern_____

Item_____ Company _____
Color/Pattern_____

Item_____ Company _____
Color/Pattern_____

ELECTRONICS

Item_____ Company _____
Color/Pattern_____

Item_____ Company _____
Color/Pattern_____

Item_____ Company _____
Color/Pattern_____

Item_____ Company _____
Color/Pattern_____

MISCELLANEOUS

Item_____ Company _____
Color/Pattern_____

Item_____ Company _____
Color/Pattern_____

Item_____ Company _____
Color/Pattern_____

Item_____ Company _____
Color/Pattern_____

HOME IMPROVEMENT PROJECT

Description of Project: _____

_____

_____

Location of Property: _____

Project Starting Date: _____ Est. Date of Completion: _____

Budgeted Amount: $_____ Actual Cost: $_____

Contracting Firm/Contractor(s): _____

_____

_____

_____

Materials Used   Cost

_____ $_____

_____ $_____

_____ $_____

_____ $_____

_____ $_____

Labor   Cost

_____ $_____

_____ $_____

_____ $_____

_____ $_____

_____ $_____

Other Details:_____

_____

Location of Receipts/Records: _____

_____

Form H601

HOMEOWNER'S VITAL DATA RECORD

Title Owner(s): _____

_____

Property Location: _____

Property Description: _____

_____

_____

_____

Date Purchased: _____ Purchase Price: $ _____

Name of Seller(s): _____

Mortgage Holder: _____

Address: _____

Phone: _____

Holder of Contract for Deed: _____

Contract Amount: $ _____ Interest Rate: _____ Due: _____

Assessed Value: $ _____ Date: _____

Location of Deed: _____

Deed Register Number: _____

Location of Property Tax Records: _____

Terms: _____

_____

_____

Other Information: _____

_____

_____

_____

HOME PROPERTY ASSESSMENTS

Item	Purchase Date	Price Paid	Current Date	Current Value
		$		$
		$		$
		$		$
		$		$
		$		$
		$		$
		$		$
		$		$
		$		$
		$		$
		$		$
		$		$
		$		$
		$		$
		$		$
		$		$
		$		$
		$		$
		$		$
		$		$
		$		$
		$		$
		$		$
		$		$
		$		$

Form H602

MAJOR PURCHASES INVENTORY

Name: _____

Item Purchased: _____

Date Purchased: _____ Purchase Location: _____

Model Number: _____ Serial Number: _____

Cost: _____ Payment Method: _____

Terms of Guarantee/Warranty: _____

For Service Call: _____ Phone: _____

Additional Information: _____

_____

Name: _____

Item Purchased: _____

Date Purchased: _____ Purchase Location: _____

Model Number: _____ Serial Number: _____

Cost: _____ Payment Method: _____

Terms of Guarantee/Warranty: _____

For Service Call: _____ Phone: _____

Additional Information: _____

_____

Name: _____

Item Purchased: _____

Date Purchased: _____ Purchase Location: _____

Model Number: _____ Serial Number: _____

Cost: _____ Payment Method: _____

Terms of Guarantee/Warranty: _____

For Service Call: _____ Phone: _____

Additional Information: _____

_____

REAL ESTATE PROPERTY WORKSHEET

Address _____

Owner name _____ Phone _____

Asking price _____

Appraisal price _____

Taxes _____

Year of completion _____

Location _____

Lot size _____

Interior space _____ sq. ft.

Style _____

Bedrooms: no., size _____

Bathrooms: no., size _____

Foundation _____

Siding _____

Roof _____

Exterior Windows & Doors _____

Garage/Shed _____

Parking Area _____

Public Utilities _____

Heating/Cooling systems _____

Fireplace _____

Insulation _____

Floor coverings _____

Wall coverings _____

Closets and storage space _____

Kitchen size, style _____

Dining room _____

Living room/Family room _____

Den/Study _____

Laundry room _____

Porch/Deck _____

Appliances _____

Expansion potential _____

Other _____

Other _____

194

Form R602

REAL ESTATE PURCHASING SCHEDULE

TASK	TARGET DATE	COMPLETION DATE
Review Ads	_____	_____
Visit Homes	_____	_____
Make an Offer	_____	_____
Sign Disclosure	_____	_____
Sign Contract	_____	_____
Deposit earnest money	_____	_____
Get home inspected	_____	_____
Resolve contingencies	_____	_____
Apply for loan	_____	_____
Loan sent to underwriting	_____	_____
Receive loan approval	_____	_____
Send commitment letter	_____	_____
Complete title work	_____	_____
Get home appraised	_____	_____
Receive appraisal results	_____	_____
Obtain hazard insurance	_____	_____
Settlement - closing statement	_____	_____

REAL ESTATE SELLING SCHEDULE

TASK	TARGET DATE	COMPLETION DATE
Place Ad	_____	_____
Open House	_____	_____
Review Offers	_____	_____
Submit Disclosure	_____	_____
Sign Contract	_____	_____
Deposit earnest money	_____	_____
Buyer's Inspection	_____	_____
Resolve contingencies	_____	_____
Buyer applies for loan	_____	_____
Buyer loan approved	_____	_____
Receive commitment letter	_____	_____
Complete title work	_____	_____
Appraisal date	_____	_____
Receive appraisal results	_____	_____
Settlement - closing statement	_____	_____

Form R604

RECORD OF SUBSCRIPTIONS

Name: _____

Name of Publication: _____

Address: _____

Phone: _____

Date Subscribed: _____ Cost: $_____ Renewal Date: _____

Length of Subscription: _____ Number of Issues: _____

Name: _____

Name of Publication: _____

Address: _____

Phone: _____

Date Subscribed: _____ Cost: $_____ Renewal Date: _____

Length of Subscription: _____ Number of Issues: _____

Name: _____

Name of Publication: _____

Address: _____

Phone: _____

Date Subscribed: _____ Cost: $_____ Renewal Date: _____

Length of Subscription: _____ Number of Issues: _____

Name: _____

Name of Publication: _____

Address: _____

Phone: _____

Date Subscribed: _____ Cost: $_____ Renewal Date: _____

Length of Subscription: _____ Number of Issues: _____

SCHEDULE OF ASSETS

Name of Testator:_____   Date of Will:_____

No.	Description of item	Form of ownership	Replacement cost
_____	_____	_____	_____
_____	_____	_____	_____
_____	_____	_____	_____
_____	_____	_____	_____
_____	_____	_____	_____
_____	_____	_____	_____
_____	_____	_____	_____
_____	_____	_____	_____
_____	_____	_____	_____
_____	_____	_____	_____
_____	_____	_____	_____
_____	_____	_____	_____
_____	_____	_____	_____
_____	_____	_____	_____
_____	_____	_____	_____
_____	_____	_____	_____
_____	_____	_____	_____
_____	_____	_____	_____
_____	_____	_____	_____
_____	_____	_____	_____
_____	_____	_____	_____

Form S601

VEHICLE MAINTENANCE SCHEDULE

Vehicle: _____

Services:	Date	Vehicle Mileage	Cost	Service Station	Next Service
Tune-up	_____	_____	$ _____	_____	_____
Tire Change	_____	_____	$ _____	_____	_____
Wheel Alignment	_____	_____	$ _____	_____	_____
Wheel Balance	_____	_____	$ _____	_____	_____
Oil Change	_____	_____	$ _____	_____	_____
Filter Change	_____	_____	$ _____	_____	_____
Battery	_____	_____	$ _____	_____	_____
Other ( )	_____	_____	$ _____	_____	_____

Additional Information: _____

_____

Vehicle: _____

Services:	Date	Vehicle Mileage	Cost	Service Station	Next Service
Tune-up	_____	_____	$ _____	_____	_____
Tire Change	_____	_____	$ _____	_____	_____
Wheel Alignment	_____	_____	$ _____	_____	_____
Wheel Balance	_____	_____	$ _____	_____	_____
Oil Change	_____	_____	$ _____	_____	_____
Filter Change	_____	_____	$ _____	_____	_____
Battery	_____	_____	$ _____	_____	_____
Other ( )	_____	_____	$ _____	_____	_____

Additional Information: _____

VEHICLE SERVICE LOG

Vehicle: _____

Owner: _____

Date	Type of Repair	Cost of Repair	Mechanic/Garage
_____	_____	$_____	_____
_____	_____	$_____	_____
_____	_____	$_____	_____
_____	_____	$_____	_____
_____	_____	$_____	_____
_____	_____	$_____	_____
_____	_____	$_____	_____
_____	_____	$_____	_____
_____	_____	$_____	_____
_____	_____	$_____	_____
_____	_____	$_____	_____
_____	_____	$_____	_____
_____	_____	$_____	_____
_____	_____	$_____	_____
_____	_____	$_____	_____
_____	_____	$_____	_____
_____	_____	$_____	_____
_____	_____	$_____	_____
_____	_____	$_____	_____

Total: $_____

Form V602

WARRANTIES ON PURCHASED PRODUCTS

Product: _____ Serial #: _____

Purchase Location: _____

Date Purchased: _____ Cost: $ _____

Warranty Terms: _____

Warrantor _____ Service Phone#:_____

Address: _____

Warranty Card/Receipt Location: _____ Exp. Date_____

Other Information: _____

Product: _____ Serial #: _____

Purchase Location: _____

Date Purchased: _____ Cost: $ _____

Warranty Terms: _____

Warrantor _____ Service Phone#:_____

Address: _____

Warranty Card/Receipt Location: _____ Exp. Date_____

Other Information: _____

Product: _____ Serial #: _____

Purchase Location: _____

Date Purchased: _____ Cost: $ _____

Warranty Terms: _____

Warrantor _____ Service Phone#:_____

Address: _____

Warranty Card/Receipt Location: _____ Exp. Date_____

Other Information: _____

Important names, dates and facts

7

Section 7

Important names, dates and facts

Forms in this section

CLUB/ORGANIZATION MEMBER LIST

Organization: _____ Date: _____

Member Name: _____ Phone: _____

Address: _____

Member Name: _____ Phone: _____

Address: _____

Member Name: _____ Phone: _____

Address: _____

Member Name: _____ Phone: _____

Address: _____

Member Name: _____ Phone: _____

Address: _____

Member Name: _____ Phone: _____

Address: _____

Member Name: _____ Phone: _____

Address: _____

Member Name: _____ Phone: _____

Address: _____

COMMONLY CALLED NUMBERS

Name

Phone

_____   _____

_____   _____

_____   _____

_____   _____

_____   _____

_____   _____

_____   _____

_____   _____

_____   _____

_____   _____

_____   _____

_____   _____

_____   _____

_____   _____

_____   _____

_____   _____

_____   _____

_____   _____

_____   _____

_____   _____

_____   _____

Form C702

CORRESPONDENCE REMINDER LIST

Name: _____

Correspond with: _____ by: _____
    Address: _____
    _____ Phone: _____
    Regarding: _____

Correspond with: _____ by: _____
    Address: _____
    _____ Phone: _____
    Regarding: _____

Correspond with: _____ by: _____
    Address: _____
    _____ Phone: _____
    Regarding: _____

Correspond with: _____ by: _____
    Address: _____
    _____ Phone: _____
    Regarding: _____

Correspond with: _____ by: _____
    Address: _____
    _____ Phone: _____
    Regarding: _____

DEATH NOTIFICATION LISTING

Name of Deceased: _____

Accountant: _____ Phone: _____

    Address: _____

Attorney: _____ Phone: _____

    Address: _____

Banker: _____ Phone: _____

    Address: _____

Clergyman/Rabbi: _____ Phone: _____

    Address: _____

(Will) Executor: _____ Phone: _____

    Address: _____

(Alternate) Executor: _____ Phone: _____

    Address: _____

Funeral Director: _____ Phone: _____

    Address: _____

Guardian: _____ Phone: _____

    Address: _____

(Contingent) Guardian: _____ Phone: _____

    Address: _____

Insurance Agent: _____ Phone: _____

    Address: _____

Insurance Underwriter: _____ Phone: _____

    Address: _____

Form D701

DIRECTORY OF PROFESSIONAL/CONSULTATION SERVICES

Name of Consultant/Service: _____

Company/Organization: _____

Address: _____

Phone: _____

Rate per Hour: _____ Availability: _____

Name of Consultant/Service: _____

Company/Organization: _____

Address: _____

Phone: _____

Rate per Hour: _____ Availability: _____

Name of Consultant/Service: _____

Company/Organization: _____

Address: _____

Phone: _____

Rate per Hour: _____ Availability: _____

Name of Consultant/Service: _____

Company/Organization: _____

Address: _____

Phone: _____

Rate per Hour: _____ Availability: _____

Name of Consultant/Service: _____

Company/Organization: _____

Address: _____

Phone: _____

Rate per Hour: _____ Availability: _____

EMERGENCY PHONE NUMBER LISTING

For: _____

Address: _____

Phone

Fire Department   _____

Police Department   _____

Hospital   _____

Physician   _____

Poison Control   _____

Ambulance   _____

Pharmacy   _____

Security Alarm Company   _____

Animal Control   _____

Work Phone Numbers   _____

_____   _____

_____   _____

Neighbors

_____   _____

_____   _____

_____   _____

Relatives

_____   _____

_____   _____

_____   _____

Form E701

IMPORTANT BIRTHDAYS

Year: _____

Celebrant	Birthdate	Age	Gift Ideas
_____	_____	_____	_____
_____	_____	_____	_____
_____	_____	_____	_____
_____	_____	_____	_____
_____	_____	_____	_____
_____	_____	_____	_____
_____	_____	_____	_____
_____	_____	_____	_____
_____	_____	_____	_____
_____	_____	_____	_____
_____	_____	_____	_____
_____	_____	_____	_____
_____	_____	_____	_____
_____	_____	_____	_____
_____	_____	_____	_____
_____	_____	_____	_____
_____	_____	_____	_____
_____	_____	_____	_____
_____	_____	_____	_____
_____	_____	_____	_____
_____	_____	_____	_____

IMPORTANT OCCASIONS TO REMEMBER

Month: _____ Year: _____

Name	Occasion	Event Date	Event Time
_____	_____	_____	_____
_____	_____	_____	_____
_____	_____	_____	_____
_____	_____	_____	_____
_____	_____	_____	_____
_____	_____	_____	_____
_____	_____	_____	_____
_____	_____	_____	_____
_____	_____	_____	_____
_____	_____	_____	_____
_____	_____	_____	_____
_____	_____	_____	_____
_____	_____	_____	_____
_____	_____	_____	_____
_____	_____	_____	_____
_____	_____	_____	_____
_____	_____	_____	_____
_____	_____	_____	_____
_____	_____	_____	_____
_____	_____	_____	_____

Form I702

IMPORTANT PHONE NUMBERS

Medical Doctor: _____ Phone: _____

    Address: _____

Veterinarian: _____ Phone: _____

    Address: _____

Pediatrician: _____ Phone: _____

    Address: _____

Hairdresser: _____ Phone: _____

    Address: _____

Manicurist: _____ Phone: _____

    Address: _____

Dentist: _____ Phone: _____

    Address: _____

Orthodontist: _____ Phone: _____

    Address: _____

Gynecologist: _____ Phone: _____

    Address: _____

Attorney: _____ Phone: _____

    Address: _____

Accountant: _____ Phone: _____

    Address: _____

Gym: _____ Phone: _____

    Address: _____

Babysitter: _____ Phone: _____

    Address: _____

Other Important Numbers: _____

_____

OFFICERS AND DIRECTORS

Organization: _____

Name	Title	Phone
_____	_____	_____
_____	_____	_____
_____	_____	_____
_____	_____	_____
_____	_____	_____

Organization: _____

Name	Title	Phone
_____	_____	_____
_____	_____	_____
_____	_____	_____
_____	_____	_____
_____	_____	_____

Organization: _____

Name	Title	Phone
_____	_____	_____
_____	_____	_____
_____	_____	_____
_____	_____	_____
_____	_____	_____

Form O701

ORGANIZATION & CLUB AFFILIATIONS

Organization: _____ Phone: _____

Address: _____

Membership Date: _____ Annual Dues: _____ Expiration Date: _____

President: _____ Phone: _____

Organization: _____ Phone: _____

Address: _____

Membership Date: _____ Annual Dues: _____ Expiration Date: _____

President: _____ Phone: _____

Organization: _____ Phone: _____

Address: _____

Membership Date: _____ Annual Dues: _____ Expiration Date: _____

President: _____ Phone: _____

Organization: _____ Phone: _____

Address: _____

Membership Date: _____ Annual Dues: _____ Expiration Date: _____

President: _____ Phone: _____

Organization: _____ Phone: _____

Address: _____

Membership Date: _____ Annual Dues: _____ Expiration Date: _____

President: _____ Phone: _____

PROGRAM PASSWORDS AND CODES

Program: Password: PIN:

_____   _____   _____
_____   _____   _____
_____   _____   _____
_____   _____   _____
_____   _____   _____
_____   _____   _____
_____   _____   _____
_____   _____   _____
_____   _____   _____
_____   _____   _____
_____   _____   _____
_____   _____   _____
_____   _____   _____
_____   _____   _____
_____   _____   _____
_____   _____   _____
_____   _____   _____
_____   _____   _____
_____   _____   _____
_____   _____   _____
_____   _____   _____
_____   _____   _____
_____   _____   _____
_____   _____   _____
_____   _____   _____

Form P701

REFERENCES

Name: _____

Reference's Name and Title: _____

_____

Home Address: _____

Phone: _____

Company Name: _____

Address: _____

Phone: _____

Used as a Reference for: _____ Date: _____

_____ Date: _____

_____ Date: _____

Reference's Name and Title: _____

_____

Home Address: _____

Phone: _____

Company Name: _____

Address: _____

Phone: _____

Used as a Reference for: _____ Date: _____

_____ Date: _____

_____ Date: _____

Event planning

Section 8

Event planning

Forms in this section

ANNOUNCEMENT GUEST LIST

Upcoming Event:_____

Host(s):_____ Announcement Date: _____

Name:_____ Phone: _____
Address: _____

Name:_____ Phone: _____
Address: _____

Name:_____ Phone: _____
Address: _____

Name:_____ Phone: _____
Address: _____

Name:_____ Phone: _____
Address: _____

Name:_____ Phone: _____
Address: _____

Name:_____ Phone: _____
Address: _____

Name:_____ Phone: _____
Address: _____

BABY SHOWER ORGANIZER

Name of New Mother: _____

Host(s): _____

Date of Shower: _____ Time of Shower: _____

Location of Shower: _____

_____

Expected Baby Delivery Date: _____ Sex of Baby:_____

Name of Baby: _____

Gift Ideas

_____   _____

_____   _____

_____   _____

_____   _____

_____   _____

Refreshment Suggestions

_____   _____

_____   _____

_____   _____

Decoration Ideas

_____   _____

_____   _____

_____   _____

Invitations

Date Sent: _____ # Sent: _____

RSVPs: # of Guests Attending: _____ # Not Attending: _____

Additional Information:_____

_____

_____

Form B801

BRIDAL SHOWER ORGANIZER

Name of Bride-to-Be: _____

Host(s): _____

Date of Shower: _____ Time of Shower: _____

Location of Shower: _____

_____

Gift Ideas

_____   _____

_____   _____

_____   _____

_____   _____

_____   _____

Refreshment Suggestions

_____   _____

_____   _____

_____   _____

Decoration Ideas

_____   _____

_____   _____

_____   _____

Invitations

Date Sent: _____ # Sent: _____

RSVPs: # of Guests Attending: _____ # Not Attending: _____

Additional Information: _____

_____

_____

FUNERAL PLANNING GUIDE

Name of Deceased: _____

Funeral Home: _____

Address: _____

Funeral Plan: _____

Director: _____ Phone: _____

Type of Service: Religious _____ Military _____ Fraternal _____

Officiator: _____ Phone: _____

Music Selections: _____

Reading Selections: _____

Flowers: _____

Memorials: _____

Pallbearers: _____

Disposition of Remains

Burial: Name of Cemetery: _____

    Location: _____

    Section: _____ Plot #: _____ Block: _____

    Deed Location: _____

    Other Instructions: _____

Cremation: Disposition of Ashes: _____

    Cremation Performed at: _____

    Other Instructions: _____

Coverage of Funeral Expenses

Life Insurance: _____

Burial Insurance: _____ Fraternal Organizations(s): _____

Social Security: _____ Veteran's Administration: _____

Pension Benefit: _____ Union Benefit: _____

Form F801

GIFT-GIVING RECORD

Name:_____ Date: _____

Gift	Date Given	Occasion	Cost	Recipient
_____	_____	_____	$ _____	_____
_____	_____	_____	$ _____	_____
_____	_____	_____	$ _____	_____
_____	_____	_____	$ _____	_____
_____	_____	_____	$ _____	_____
_____	_____	_____	$ _____	_____
_____	_____	_____	$ _____	_____
_____	_____	_____	$ _____	_____
_____	_____	_____	$ _____	_____
_____	_____	_____	$ _____	_____
_____	_____	_____	$ _____	_____
_____	_____	_____	$ _____	_____
_____	_____	_____	$ _____	_____
_____	_____	_____	$ _____	_____
_____	_____	_____	$ _____	_____
_____	_____	_____	$ _____	_____
_____	_____	_____	$ _____	_____
_____	_____	_____	$ _____	_____
_____	_____	_____	$ _____	_____
_____	_____	_____	$ _____	_____
_____	_____	_____	$ _____	_____
_____	_____	_____	$ _____	_____
_____	_____	_____	$ _____	_____
_____	_____	_____	$ _____	_____

GUEST INVITATION REGISTRY

Occasion: _____

Date of Occasion: _____ Time: _____

Location: _____

Guest   Address

_____   _____

_____   _____

_____   _____

_____   _____

_____   _____

_____   _____

_____   _____

_____   _____

_____   _____

_____   _____

_____   _____

_____   _____

_____   _____

_____   _____

_____   _____

_____   _____

_____   _____

Form G802

INVITATION RESPONSE FORM

Event: _____ Date: _____

Guest(s) Invited	Phone	RSVP	RSVP Date
_____	_____	_____	_____
_____	_____	_____	_____
_____	_____	_____	_____
_____	_____	_____	_____
_____	_____	_____	_____
_____	_____	_____	_____
_____	_____	_____	_____
_____	_____	_____	_____
_____	_____	_____	_____
_____	_____	_____	_____
_____	_____	_____	_____
_____	_____	_____	_____
_____	_____	_____	_____
_____	_____	_____	_____
_____	_____	_____	_____
_____	_____	_____	_____
_____	_____	_____	_____
_____	_____	_____	_____
_____	_____	_____	_____
_____	_____	_____	_____
_____	_____	_____	_____

PARTY PLANNING RECORD

Occasion: _____ Guest(s) of Honor: _____

Host(s): _____

Party Date: _____ Time: _____

Party Location: _____

Gift Ideas

_____   _____

_____   _____

_____   _____

_____   _____

_____   _____

Refreshment Suggestions

_____   _____

_____   _____

_____   _____

_____   _____

Decoration Ideas

_____   _____

_____   _____

_____   _____

_____   _____

Invitations

Date Sent: _____ # Sent: _____

RSVPs: # of Guests Attending: _____ # Not Attending: _____

Additional Information: _____

_____

_____

DAILY PROJECT LIST

Date:_____

HIGH PRIORITY	DATE DUE	COMPLETED
1.		
2.		
3.		
4.		
5.		
6.		
7.		
8.		
9.		
10.		

LOW PRIORITY	DATE DUE	COMPLETED
1.		
2.		
3.		
4.		
5.		
6.		
7.		
8.		
9.		
10.		

RELIGIOUS EVENTS

Event:_____

Date: _____ Time: _____ Place:_____

Name of Clergyman:_____

In Attendance

_____   _____   _____
_____   _____   _____
_____   _____   _____
_____   _____   _____
_____   _____   _____
_____   _____   _____
_____   _____   _____
_____   _____   _____
_____   _____   _____
_____   _____   _____
_____   _____   _____
_____   _____   _____
_____   _____   _____
_____   _____   _____
_____   _____   _____

Additional Information:_____

_____

Form R801

SPECIAL DINNER PARTY PLANNER

Host(s): _____

Location: _____

Date: _____ Time: _____

Dinner Party Guest(s)

_____ _____ _____

_____ _____ _____

_____ _____ _____

_____ _____ _____

_____ _____ _____

Dinner Served

Cocktails: _____

Appetizer: _____

Salad: _____

Wine: _____

Entree: _____

Side Dishes: _____

Dessert: _____

Coffee: _____

Liqueurs/Cordials: _____

Music: _____

Flowers: _____

Table Arrangement: _____

Guests' Allergies/Dislikes: _____

_____

Special Diet Options: _____

_____

Travel data

Section 9

Travel data

Forms in this section

FAMILY TRAVEL BUDGET

NAME _____ PERIOD _____ ,2_____ TO _____ , 2____

DAY	MONDAY	TUESDAY	WEDNESDAY	THURSDAY	FRIDAY	SATURDAY	SUNDAY	TOTALS
DATE								
CITY								
HOTEL								
MILEAGE @_____								
LAUNDRY								
BREAKFAST								
LUNCH								
DINNER								
OTHER								
TRANSPORT								
TAXI								
TIPS								
CAR RENTAL								
GAS & OIL								
PARKING								
TELE/FAX								
POSTAGE								
ENTERTAIN								
GIFTS								
SOUVENIRS								
TOTALS								

SPECIAL NOTES:

LOG OF FREQUENT FLYER MILES

Name: _____ Frequent Flyer #_____

Airline: _____

Date	From	To	Ticket #	Miles	Total Miles
_____	_____	_____	_____	_____	_____
_____	_____	_____	_____	_____	_____
_____	_____	_____	_____	_____	_____
_____	_____	_____	_____	_____	_____
_____	_____	_____	_____	_____	_____
_____	_____	_____	_____	_____	_____
_____	_____	_____	_____	_____	_____
_____	_____	_____	_____	_____	_____
_____	_____	_____	_____	_____	_____
_____	_____	_____	_____	_____	_____
_____	_____	_____	_____	_____	_____
_____	_____	_____	_____	_____	_____
_____	_____	_____	_____	_____	_____
_____	_____	_____	_____	_____	_____
_____	_____	_____	_____	_____	_____
_____	_____	_____	_____	_____	_____
_____	_____	_____	_____	_____	_____
_____	_____	_____	_____	_____	_____
_____	_____	_____	_____	_____	_____

Total: _____

Form L901

NAUTICAL LOG

Boat/Ship Name: _____

Docked at:_____

Cruise Date:_____ Destination: _____

Time Departed:_____ Time Returned: _____ Fuel: _____

Weather Conditions: _____

Sea Conditions: _____

Passengers

_____   _____

_____   _____

_____   _____

_____   _____

_____   _____

_____   _____

_____   _____

_____   _____

Additional Comments:_____

_____

_____

_____

_____

_____

_____

_____

_____

_____

PASSPORT LISTING

Name: _____

Passport #:_____ Country: _____

Date Issued:_____ Expiration Date: _____

Issuing Authority: _____

Location of Passport: _____

Additional Information:_____

_____

Name: _____

Passport #:_____ Country: _____

Date Issued:_____ Expiration Date: _____

Issuing Authority: _____

Location of Passport: _____

Additional Information:_____

_____

Name: _____

Passport #:_____ Country: _____

Date Issued:_____ Expiration Date: _____

Issuing Authority: _____

Location of Passport: _____

Additional Information:_____

_____

PLACES TO GO

Name:_____ Date: _____

Ideas	Name	Location	Cost:
Museums:	_____	_____	$ _____
Nature Parks:	_____	_____	$ _____
Zoos:	_____	_____	$ _____
Amusement Parks:	_____	_____	$ _____
Famous Buildings:	_____	_____	$ _____
Monuments:	_____	_____	$ _____
Rivers:	_____	_____	$ _____
Lakes:	_____	_____	$ _____
Oceans:	_____	_____	$ _____
Famous Sights:	_____	_____	$ _____
Places to Eat:	_____	_____	$ _____
Concerts:	_____	_____	$ _____
Clubs:	_____	_____	$ _____
Festivals:	_____	_____	$ _____
Arts & Crafts Fairs:	_____	_____	$ _____
Spectator Sports:	_____	_____	$ _____
Participatory Sports:	_____	_____	$ _____
Shopping Centers:	_____	_____	$ _____
Other(s):	_____	_____	$ _____
	_____	_____	$ _____
	_____	_____	$ _____
	_____	_____	$ _____
	_____	_____	$ _____
	_____	_____	$ _____

PLANE/BOAT OWNERSHIP RECORD

Owner's Name: _____ Date Purchased: _____

Purchase Price: _____

Registration #: _____ Registration Date: _____

Purchased from: _____ ID #: _____

Make: _____ Model: _____ Year: _____

Physical Description: _____

_____

_____

_____

Dock/Storage Location: _____

_____

Insured by: _____ Insured Value: $ _____

Liability: $ _____ Contact: _____

Additional Information: _____

_____

_____

_____

_____

_____

_____

_____

_____

_____

_____

_____

TRAVEL AGENDA

Name: _____

Date: _____

Hotel: _____

Location: _____ Phone: _____

Scheduled Appointments/Events: _____

_____

Additional Information: _____

Date: _____

Hotel: _____

Location: _____ Phone: _____

Scheduled Appointments/Events: _____

_____

Additional Information: _____

Date: _____

Hotel: _____

Location: _____ Phone: _____

Scheduled Appointments/Events: _____

_____

Additional Information: _____

Date: _____

Hotel: _____

Location: _____ Phone: _____

Scheduled Appointments/Events: _____

_____

Additional Information: _____

TRAVEL CHECKLIST

Name: _____

Destination: _____

Date of Trip: _____ Length of Trip: _____

Personal Items

_____   _____   _____

_____   _____   _____

_____   _____   _____

Clothing

_____   _____   _____

_____   _____   _____

_____   _____   _____

_____   _____   _____

Business Items

_____   _____   _____

_____   _____   _____

_____   _____   _____

_____   _____   _____

Gifts

_____   _____   _____

_____   _____   _____

_____   _____   _____

Miscellaneous

_____   _____   _____

_____   _____   _____

_____   _____   _____

Form T902

TRAVEL ITINERARY

Name: _____

Destination: _____

Trip Date: _____ to _____

Flight Information

Departure Date: _____ Departure Time: _____

Location: _____

Airline: _____ Flight #: _____ Gate #: _____

Arrival Time: _____ Location: _____

Return Date: _____ Return: _____

Location: _____

Airline: _____ Flight #: _____ Gate #: _____

Arrival Time: _____ Location: _____

Hotel Information

Hotel: _____ Phone #: _____

Address: _____

Date(s) Room Reserved: _____

Bus/Train Information: _____

_____

Rental Car Information: _____

_____

Appointments/Events Scheduled: _____

_____

Important Phone #s: _____

Additional Information: _____

_____

_____

VACATION LOG

Place Visited: _____

    Location: _____ Date: from _____ to _____

    Purpose: _____

    People in Party: _____

    Sights Seen: _____

    _____

    Additional Comments/Special Moments: _____

    _____

Place Visited: _____

    Location: _____ Date: from _____ to _____

    Purpose: _____

    People in Party: _____

    Sights Seen: _____

    _____

    Additional Comments/Special Moments: _____

    _____

Place Visited: _____

    Location: _____ Date: from _____ to _____

    Purpose: _____

    People in Party: _____

    Sights Seen: _____

    _____

    Additional Comments/Special Moments: _____

    _____

Form V901

TRAVEL VISA RECORD

Name: _____

Type of Visa: _____ Visa #: _____

Issued: _____ Country: _____ Expires: _____

Issued by: _____

Visa Location: _____

Additional Information: _____

_____

_____

Name: _____

Type of Visa: _____ Visa #: _____

Issued: _____ Country: _____ Expires: _____

Issued by: _____

Visa Location: _____

Additional Information: _____

_____

_____

Name: _____

Type of Visa: _____ Visa #: _____

Issued: _____ Country: _____ Expires: _____

Issued by: _____

Visa Location: _____

Additional Information: _____

_____

_____

VEHICLE TRIP RECORD

FOR THE MONTH OF _____, 2____

VEHICLE NUMBER_____ LICENSE NUMBER_____

	EXPENSES				TRIP RECORD
Day	Miles /KM	Gas Oil	Repairs	Tolls & Parking	
1.					
2.					
3.					
4.					
5.					
6.					
7.					
8.					
9.					
10.					
11.					
12.					
13.					
14.					
15.					
16.					
17.					
18.					
19.					
20.					
21.					
22.					
23.					
24.					
25.					
26.					
27.					
28.					
29.					
30.					
31.					
Totals					

ADDITIONAL COMMENTS:

_____
OPERATOR'S SIGNATURE

Form V903

Recreational activities

10

Section 10

Recreational activities

Forms in this section

BOOK LIST

Name:_____ Date: _____

Title of Book: _____

Type of Book: _____

Author:_____ Date Read: _____

Comments: _____

_____

Other Books by this Author: _____

_____

Title of Book: _____

Type of Book: _____

Author:_____ Date Read: _____

Comments: _____

_____

Other Books by this Author: _____

_____

Title of Book: _____

Type of Book: _____

Author:_____ Date Read: _____

Comments: _____

_____

Other Books by this Author: _____

_____

COMPUTER PROBLEMS DIARY

Date: _____

Nature of Problem: _____

_____

Tech Support Contacted: _____   Date Contacted: _____

Solution Given: _____

_____

Notes: _____

_____

Date: _____

Nature of Problem: _____

_____

Tech Support Contacted: _____   Date Contacted: _____

Solution Given: _____

_____

Notes: _____

_____

Date: _____

Nature of Problem: _____

_____

Tech Support Contacted: _____   Date Contacted: _____

Solution Given: _____

_____

Notes: _____

_____

Form C110

COMPUTER UPGRADE RECORD

Program: _____   Format: _____

Tech Support Number: _____   Company: _____

Last Version: _____   Date Purchased: _____

Place of Purchase: _____   Date Installed: _____

Problems: _____

Current Version: _____   Date Purchased: _____

Place of Purchase: _____   Date Installed: _____

Comments: _____

Program: _____   Format: _____

Tech Support Number: _____   Company: _____

Last Version: _____   Date Purchased: _____

Place of Purchase: _____   Date Installed: _____

Problems: _____

Current Version: _____   Date Purchased: _____

Place of Purchase: _____   Date Installed: _____

Comments: _____

Program: _____   Format: _____

Tech Support Number: _____   Company: _____

Last Version: _____   Date Purchased: _____

Place of Purchase: _____   Date Installed: _____

Problems: _____

Current Version: _____   Date Purchased: _____

Place of Purchase: _____   Date Installed: _____

Comments: _____

E-MAIL ADDRESS LIST

Name:	E-mail address:	Telephone/Fax:

LIBRARY OF MUSIC

Name:_____ Date: _____

Item #	Title	Artist	Format (tape, record or CD)
_____	_____	_____	_____
_____	_____	_____	_____
_____	_____	_____	_____
_____	_____	_____	_____
_____	_____	_____	_____
_____	_____	_____	_____
_____	_____	_____	_____
_____	_____	_____	_____
_____	_____	_____	_____
_____	_____	_____	_____
_____	_____	_____	_____
_____	_____	_____	_____
_____	_____	_____	_____
_____	_____	_____	_____
_____	_____	_____	_____
_____	_____	_____	_____
_____	_____	_____	_____
_____	_____	_____	_____
_____	_____	_____	_____

Code for Format: C = Cassette Tape   CD = Compact Disc   R = Record

MOVIE LOG AND REVIEW

Title of Movie	Date Viewed	Type	Rating
_____	_____	_____	_____
_____	_____	_____	_____
_____	_____	_____	_____
_____	_____	_____	_____
_____	_____	_____	_____
_____	_____	_____	_____
_____	_____	_____	_____
_____	_____	_____	_____
_____	_____	_____	_____
_____	_____	_____	_____
_____	_____	_____	_____
_____	_____	_____	_____
_____	_____	_____	_____
_____	_____	_____	_____
_____	_____	_____	_____
_____	_____	_____	_____
_____	_____	_____	_____
_____	_____	_____	_____
_____	_____	_____	_____
_____	_____	_____	_____
_____	_____	_____	_____
_____	_____	_____	_____
_____	_____	_____	_____
_____	_____	_____	_____
_____	_____	_____	_____
_____	_____	_____	_____
_____	_____	_____	_____
_____	_____	_____	_____

Form M110

ROSTER OF SPORTING RESULTS

Name: _____

Sport: _____ Team: _____

Date	Rival Team	Location of Game	Score	Record to Date
_____	_____	_____	_____	_____
_____	_____	_____	_____	_____
_____	_____	_____	_____	_____
_____	_____	_____	_____	_____
_____	_____	_____	_____	_____
_____	_____	_____	_____	_____
_____	_____	_____	_____	_____
_____	_____	_____	_____	_____
_____	_____	_____	_____	_____
_____	_____	_____	_____	_____
_____	_____	_____	_____	_____
_____	_____	_____	_____	_____
_____	_____	_____	_____	_____
_____	_____	_____	_____	_____
_____	_____	_____	_____	_____
_____	_____	_____	_____	_____
_____	_____	_____	_____	_____
_____	_____	_____	_____	_____
_____	_____	_____	_____	_____
_____	_____	_____	_____	_____

SOFTWARE INVENTORY

Title:	Format:	Date Purchased:	Comments:

Form S110

TV/VCR RECORDING SCHEDULE

Name: _____

Week of: _____

	Time	Program	Channel	Hours
Sunday:	_____	_____	_____	_____
	_____	_____	_____	_____
	_____	_____	_____	_____
Monday:	_____	_____	_____	_____
	_____	_____	_____	_____
	_____	_____	_____	_____
Tuesday:	_____	_____	_____	_____
	_____	_____	_____	_____
	_____	_____	_____	_____
Wednesday	_____	_____	_____	_____
	_____	_____	_____	_____
	_____	_____	_____	_____
Thursday	_____	_____	_____	_____
	_____	_____	_____	_____
	_____	_____	_____	_____
Friday:	_____	_____	_____	_____
	_____	_____	_____	_____
	_____	_____	_____	_____
Saturday	_____	_____	_____	_____
	_____	_____	_____	_____
	_____	_____	_____	_____

Total Hours: _____

UPCOMING ENTERTAINMENT ATTRACTIONS

Name: _____

Month: _____ Year: _____

Event	Location	Date	Cost
Theatre:			
_____	_____	_____	$_____
_____	_____	_____	$_____
_____	_____	_____	$_____
Arts:			
_____	_____	_____	$_____
_____	_____	_____	$_____
_____	_____	_____	$_____
Movies:			
_____	_____	_____	$_____
_____	_____	_____	$_____
_____	_____	_____	$_____
Concerts:			
_____	_____	_____	$_____
_____	_____	_____	$_____
_____	_____	_____	$_____
Festivals/Fairs:			
_____	_____	_____	$_____
_____	_____	_____	$_____
_____	_____	_____	$_____
Specialty/Trade Shows:			
_____	_____	_____	$_____
_____	_____	_____	$_____
_____	_____	_____	$_____

Form U110

VIDEOCASSETTE REGISTRY

Name:_____Date: _____

Tape #	Video Title	Type of Movie (comedy, etc.)	Running Time
_____	_____	_____	_____
_____	_____	_____	_____
_____	_____	_____	_____
_____	_____	_____	_____
_____	_____	_____	_____
_____	_____	_____	_____
_____	_____	_____	_____
_____	_____	_____	_____
_____	_____	_____	_____
_____	_____	_____	_____
_____	_____	_____	_____
_____	_____	_____	_____
_____	_____	_____	_____
_____	_____	_____	_____
_____	_____	_____	_____
_____	_____	_____	_____
_____	_____	_____	_____
_____	_____	_____	_____
_____	_____	_____	_____
_____	_____	_____	_____

VIDEOGAME COLLECTION

Name:_____Date: _____

Cartridge Name   Item #   Location

_____   _____   _____

_____   _____   _____

_____   _____   _____

_____   _____   _____

_____   _____   _____

_____   _____   _____

_____   _____   _____

_____   _____   _____

_____   _____   _____

_____   _____   _____

_____   _____   _____

_____   _____   _____

_____   _____   _____

_____   _____   _____

_____   _____   _____

_____   _____   _____

_____   _____   _____

_____   _____   _____

_____   _____   _____

_____   _____   _____

_____   _____   _____

Form V210

WEB SITE ADDRESS LIST

Web Address: Description:

_____   _____

_____   _____

_____   _____

_____   _____

_____   _____

_____   _____

_____   _____

_____   _____

_____   _____

_____   _____

_____   _____

_____   _____

_____   _____

_____   _____

_____   _____

_____   _____

_____   _____

_____   _____

_____   _____

_____   _____

_____   _____

_____   _____

_____   _____

Special projects

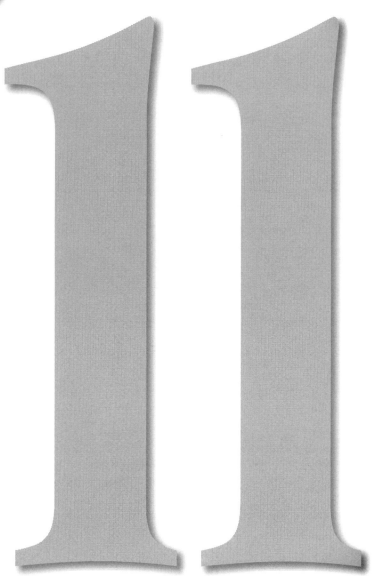

Section 11
Special projects

Forms in this section

ACTIVITY PLANNER - MONTHLY

Name: _____

Month of: _____ Year: _____

Date   Time   Activity

_____   _____   _____

_____   _____   _____

_____   _____   _____

_____   _____   _____

_____   _____   _____

_____   _____   _____

_____   _____   _____

_____   _____   _____

_____   _____   _____

_____   _____   _____

_____   _____   _____

_____   _____   _____

_____   _____   _____

_____   _____   _____

_____   _____   _____

_____   _____   _____

_____   _____   _____

_____   _____   _____

_____   _____   _____

_____   _____   _____

ACTIVITY PLANNER - WEEKLY

Name: _____

Week of: _____ Year: _____

Date   Time   Activity

_____   _____   _____

_____   _____   _____

_____   _____   _____

_____   _____   _____

_____   _____   _____

_____   _____   _____

_____   _____   _____

_____   _____   _____

_____   _____   _____

_____   _____   _____

_____   _____   _____

_____   _____   _____

_____   _____   _____

_____   _____   _____

_____   _____   _____

_____   _____   _____

_____   _____   _____

_____   _____   _____

_____   _____   _____

Form A211

CLIENT'S RECORD OF CHARGES

	PERSON	HOURLY CHARGES	HOURS	TOTAL	PAID	BALANCE DUE
7:00						
7:15						
7:30						
7:45						
8:00						
8:15						
8:30						
8:45						
9:00						
9:15						
9:30						
9:45						
10:00						
10:15						
10:30						
10:45						
11:00						
11:15						
11:30						
11:45						
12:00						
12:15						
12:30						
12:45						
1:00						
1:15						
1:30						
1:45						
2:00						
2:15						
2:30						
2:45						
3:00						
3:15						
3:30						
3:45						
4:00						
4:15						
4:30						
4:45						
5:00						
5:15						
5:30						
5:45						
6:00						
6:15						
6:30						
6:45						
7:00						

Form C111

MONTHLY GOALS

Name:_____ Year:_____

	Goal	Date to be Completed
January	_____	_____
	_____	_____
February	_____	_____
	_____	_____
March	_____	_____
	_____	_____
April	_____	_____
	_____	_____
May	_____	_____
	_____	_____
June	_____	_____
	_____	_____
July	_____	_____
	_____	_____
August	_____	_____
	_____	_____
September	_____	_____
	_____	_____
October	_____	_____
	_____	_____
November	_____	_____
	_____	_____
December	_____	_____
	_____	_____

Form M111

PERSONAL GOALS

Name:_____ Date: _____

For today: _____

_____

_____

_____

For this week: _____

_____

_____

_____

For this month: _____

_____

_____

_____

For this year: _____

_____

_____

_____

To accomplish within 5 years:_____

_____

_____

To accomplish within a decade: _____

_____

_____

To accomplish within a lifetime:_____

_____

_____

PLANS FOR FUTURE PROJECTS

Name of Project Planner: _____

Date: _____

Project Concept: _____

Steps Taken to Date: _____

_____

Future Steps: _____

_____

Name of Project Planner: _____

Date: _____

Project Concept: _____

Steps Taken to Date: _____

_____

Future Steps: _____

_____

Name of Project Planner: _____

Date: _____

Project Concept: _____

Steps Taken to Date: _____

_____

Future Steps: _____

_____

Form P211

PROJECT UPDATE

Name: _____

Type of Project: _____

Start Date: _____ Target Date: _____ Completed: _____

Steps Taken to Date: _____

_____

_____

Future Steps: _____

_____

_____

Comments/Suggestions: _____

_____

_____

Name: _____

Type of Project: _____

Start Date: _____ Target Date: _____ Completed: _____

Steps Taken to Date: _____

_____

_____

Future Steps: _____

_____

_____

Comments/Suggestions: _____

_____

_____

REQUISITION FOR PRINTING

TO: DATE: _____
                                    P.O. NUMBER: _____

JOB TITLE: _____

○   PHOTOCOPY SERVICE   ○   OFFSET

NUMBER OF PAGES [   ]   NUMBER OF COPIES [   ]

PAPER SIZE: ❏ 8$\frac{1}{2}$" X 11"   ❏ 8$\frac{1}{2}$" X 14"   ❏ 11" X 17"

PLEASE PRINT: ❏ 1 SIDE   ❏ 2 SIDES   ❏ TUMBLED

              ❏ CUT   ❏ FOLD   ❏ PADDED

ADDITIONAL SPECIFICATIONS OR SPECIAL INSTRUCTIONS:

_____
_____
_____
_____
_____

REQUESTED DELIVERY DATE: _____

CONTACT: _____ TELE: _____

COMPANY: _____

ADDRESS: _____

_____

APPROVED BY: _____

Form R111

SCHEDULE OF PROJECTS

Name:_____ Date: _____

Project: _____
Estim. Completion Date: _____ Actual Completion Date: _____

Project: _____
Estim. Completion Date: _____ Actual Completion Date: _____

Project: _____
Estim. Completion Date: _____ Actual Completion Date: _____

Project: _____
Estim. Completion Date: _____ Actual Completion Date: _____

Project: _____
Estim. Completion Date: _____ Actual Completion Date: _____

Project: _____
Estim. Completion Date: _____ Actual Completion Date: _____

Project: _____
Estim. Completion Date: _____ Actual Completion Date: _____

Project: _____
Estim. Completion Date: _____ Actual Completion Date: _____

SIX-MONTH GOALS

Name:_____ Date: _____

Goal	Date Achieved	Comments
_____	_____	_____
_____	_____	_____
_____	_____	_____
_____	_____	_____
_____	_____	_____
_____	_____	_____
_____	_____	_____
_____	_____	_____
_____	_____	_____
_____	_____	_____
_____	_____	_____
_____	_____	_____
_____	_____	_____
_____	_____	_____
_____	_____	_____
_____	_____	_____
_____	_____	_____
_____	_____	_____
_____	_____	_____

Form S211

THREE-MONTH GOALS

Name:_____ Date: _____

Goal	Date Achieved	Comments
_____	_____	_____
_____	_____	_____
_____	_____	_____
_____	_____	_____
_____	_____	_____
_____	_____	_____
_____	_____	_____
_____	_____	_____
_____	_____	_____
_____	_____	_____
_____	_____	_____
_____	_____	_____
_____	_____	_____
_____	_____	_____
_____	_____	_____
_____	_____	_____
_____	_____	_____
_____	_____	_____
_____	_____	_____
_____	_____	_____

WEEKLY OBJECTIVES

Name:_____ Week of: _____

	Objective	Comments
Sunday:	_____	_____
	_____	_____
	_____	_____
Monday:	_____	_____
	_____	_____
	_____	_____
Tuesday:	_____	_____
	_____	_____
	_____	_____
Wednesday:	_____	_____
	_____	_____
	_____	_____
	_____	_____
Thursday:	_____	_____
	_____	_____
	_____	_____
Friday:	_____	_____
	_____	_____
	_____	_____
Saturday:	_____	_____
	_____	_____
	_____	_____

Form W111

Resources

••• Online Resources •••

◆ **American Council on Education**

http://www.acenet.edu

◆ **American Medical Association Health Insight**

http://www.ama-assn.org/consumer.htm

◆ **Automotive Learning On-Line**

http://www.innerbody.com/innerauto/htm/auto.html

◆ **Ancestry.com, Inc.**

http://ancestry.ldsworld.com

◆ **Appoint.Net Inc.**

http://www.appoint.net/cal/default.asp?r=1

◆ **Center for the Study of Services**

http://consumer.checkbook.org/consumer

◆ **College Is Possible**

http://www.collegeispossible.org

◆ **College Savings Plans Network National Association of State Treasurers.**

http://www.collegesavings.org/Default.htm

◆ **Consumer Information Center of the U.S. General Services Administration**

http://www.pueblo.gsa.gov

◆ **Consumer World**

http://www.consumerworld.org

◆ **Debt Counselors of America**

http://www.dca.org/

◆ **Desk Reference**

http://www.deskreference.com

◆ **Destinations - Your Vacation Travel Guide**

http://www.detroitnewspapers.com/destinations/webclass1.asp

- **Excite Family**

  http://www.excite.com/family

- **EXES Travel Search**

  http://www.exes.com

- **Federal Resources for Educational Excellence (FREE)**

  http://www.ed.gov/free

- **Federal Trade Commission**

  http://www.ftc.gov

- **Great Outdoor Recreation Pages**

  http://www.gorp.com

- **Health Care Financing Administration (HCFA)**

  http://www.hcfa.gov/

- **Human Anatomy On-Line**

  http://www.innerbody.com

- **Idea Cafe**

  http://www.ideacafe.com

- **Inc. Online**

  http://www.inc.com

◆ **Insurance Information Institute**

http://www.iii.org

◆ **Interactive Pregnancy Calendar by Parents Place.com**

http://www.pregnancycalendar.com/

◆ **Internet Wedding Links Global Search**

http://a-wedding.com

◆ **Mapquest**

http://www.mapquest.com

◆ **National Fraud Information Center**

http://www.fraud.org

◆ **National Park Service**

http://www.nps.gov/parks.html

◆ **NCSU Cooperative Extension—How Long Should Records Be Kept?**

http://gaston.ces.state.nc.us/staff/howlong.html

◆ **Online Vacation Mall**

http://onlinevacationmall.com

◆ **Recreation.Gov**

http://www.recreation.gov

◆ **Remind U-Mail**

http://calendar.stwing.upenn.edu

◆ **Shape Up America!**

http://www.shapeup.org

◆ **Small Business Exchange American Express Company**

http://www.americanexpress.com/smallbusiness/default.asp?

◆ **Social Security Online**

http://www.ssa.gov/SSA_Home.html

◆ **Surf and Sun - "Beach Vacation Guide"**

http://www.surf-sun.com

◆ **Tax and Accounting Sites Directory**

http://www.taxsites.com

◆ **Travelocity**

http://www.travelocity.com

◆ **U.S. Department of Education**

   http://www.ed.gov

◆ **U.S. Department of Health and Human Services Healthfinder**

   http://www.healthfinder.gov

◆ **U.S. Business Advisor**

   http://www.business.gov

◆ **WebCrawler Kids & Family**

   http://webcrawler.com/kids_and_family/

◆ **Yahoo! Address Book**

   http://address.yahoo.com

◆ **Yahoo! Calendar**

   http://calendar.yahoo.com